NATIONAL-LOUIS UNIVERSITY
371.1038153P
C002
PARENT-TEACHER CONFERENCES NEW

O9-ABG-314

3 2842 1802 7332 5

WITHDRAWN

Parent-
Teacher
Conferences

McGraw-Hill
Series in
Education

Harold Benjamin Consulting Editor-in-Chief

ARNO A. BELLACK *Teachers College, Columbia University*
CONSULTING EDITOR, CURRICULUM AND METHODS IN EDUCATION

HAROLD BENJAMIN *Emeritus Professor of Education*
George Peabody College for Teachers
CONSULTING EDITOR, FOUNDATIONS IN EDUCATION

HARLAN HAGMAN *Wayne State University*
CONSULTING EDITOR, ADMINISTRATION IN EDUCATION

NICHOLAS HOBBS *George Peabody College for Teachers*
CONSULTING EDITOR, PSYCHOLOGY
AND HUMAN DEVELOPMENT IN EDUCATION

WALTER F. JOHNSON *Michigan State University*
CONSULTING EDITOR, GUIDANCE, COUNSELING,
AND STUDENT PERSONNEL IN EDUCATION

Guidance, Counseling, and Student Personnel in Education

Walter F. Johnson Consulting Editor

Bailard and Strang, Parent-Teacher Conferences
Bennett, Guidance and Counseling in Groups
Berdie, Testing in Guidance and Counseling
Detjen and Detjen, Elementary School Guidance
Hoppock, Occupational Information
Johnson, Stefflre, and Edelfelt, Pupil Personnel
and Guidance Services
Jones, Principles of Guidance
Warters, Techniques of Counseling

Parent-
Teacher
Conferences

Virginia Bailard

Supervisor of Counseling and
Psychological Services
Long Beach Unified School District
Long Beach, California

Ruth Strang

Professor of Education
University of Arizona
Tucson, Arizona

WITHDRAWN

McGraw-Hill Book Company, Inc.

New York   San Francisco   Toronto   London

NATIONAL COLLEGE OF EDUCATION
LIBRARY
EVANSTON, ILLINOIS

371.103
B153p

Parent-Teacher Conferences

Copyright © 1964 by the McGraw-Hill Book Company, Inc.
All Rights Reserved.
Printed in the United States of America.
This book, or parts thereof, may not be reproduced in any form
without permission of the publishers.
Library of Congress Catalog Card Number: 63–15887

57256

03056

Preface

Interest in parent-teacher conferences is increasing. From incidental contacts, mostly concerning discipline problems, these conferences have developed into one of the most effective means of reporting pupil progress and of understanding the child in his environment. Although not so common in high school as in elementary school, they are equally important in the guidance of adolescents.

The aim of this book is to help teachers to do better the parent-teacher conference work they are now doing. To accomplish this purpose, the parent-teacher conference is first presented as a process of two-way communication between parent and teacher. Next the conference is placed in its setting of total parent education. Another phase of parent education, namely, group work with parents, is described in a separate chapter. Since the success of parent-teacher conferences depends a great deal on proper scheduling, preliminary preparation, skillful interviewing, and evaluation leading to improvement, Chapter 4 is devoted to the problems of mechanics and techniques. In this chapter, some of the special problems of conducting parent-teacher conferences in high school are also considered.

Since parent-teacher conferences take many forms and have quite different content, the remaining chapters deal with a number of typical conference situations: the unscheduled conference initiated by the parent; systematically scheduled conferences regarding the child's school progress, which supplement and, especially in the lower grades, are a substitute for the report card; important conferences with parents of preschool children to help them make the preschool years a prelude to school success; and conferences involving a discussion of reading problems, about which many parents are greatly concerned.

Other conferences are held with the parents of all the pupils in the school, and at certain times the teacher will talk with parents of the gifted and of children showing different degrees of mental retardation. Problems of educational and vocational guidance loom large in the conference with parents of high school students, and some complex problems require home visits and concerted action, for which teachers have neither time nor preparation. In these cases the psychologist, counselor, or school social worker may conduct the interview. Several conferences are included to acquaint teachers with the specialized services that may be available and to give teachers suggestions as to techniques and interpretation which may help them to conduct their parent conferences more effectively.

Each of the chapters dealing with different kinds of parent-teacher conferences attempts to give (1) some background knowledge about the special kind of problem, (2) help with interviewing techniques, and (3) illustrations from actual parent-teacher conferences. The reader should remember that the illustrations given are only excerpts from more complete interviews and that they do not convey the nonverbal communication effected through tone of voice, facial expression, and bodily movements which makes much of the difference between a successful and an unsuccessful conference. In reading interview material, the reader should also be aware of the differences in parents— some overready to go along with anything the teacher says; others genuinely appreciative of the teacher's interest in their child; and still others verbally agreeing but with many unexpressed reservations. The reader would profit greatly by putting himself in the interviewer's place and thinking what he would say in response to each of the parents' comments.

The authors have felt the need for a book of this kind in guidance classes, in courses in counseling techniques and elementary and secondary education methods, in workshops for teachers, in school professional libraries, as well as in classes and school situations in which the focus is specifically on parent-teacher conferences.

Grateful acknowledgment for assistance in supplying interview material and descriptions of programs and procedures for this book is made to Mrs. Hazel Huston, School Psychologist, Mrs. Marye G. Spencer, School Social Worker, Mrs. Javus Fortmann, Principal, Webster Elementary School, and Miss Marion Wells, Principal, Lowell Elementary School, all of Long Beach Unified School District, Long Beach, California; and Miss Catherine Paulsen, Director of Guidance, Taft Union High School, Taft, California.

Virginia Bailard

Ruth Strang

Contents

Contents

Communication between parents and teachers

CHAPTER ONE

Teachers' understanding of parents   Parents' understanding of teachers
Approaches to parents   Having facts to communicate   Nonverbal com-
munication   Verbal communication   Speaking their language   Being
simple and concrete   Speaking effectively   Personalizing communication

Parent-teacher conferences are teachers' best means of communicating with parents. In this face-to-face relation, information and ideas about the child are exchanged, insight is gained, attitudes are caught, and plans for furthering his best development are evolved. From preschool years through high school, skillfully conducted conferences with parents have been enlightening to parents and teachers and beneficial to children and adolescents. They are part of the modern teacher's responsibility.

The communication process is the core of the parent conference. Communication may be verbal or nonverbal. Words, understood by both parent and teacher, convey thoughts, ideas, and insights. A smile, a nod, a bodily attitude of paying close attention convey interest, concern, and approval. Communication is the basic purpose of parent-teacher conferences.

Underlying the communication process are mutual understanding, respect, and appreciation. The teacher understands some of the parents' problems in bringing up children. The parent realizes the teacher's difficulties in meeting the needs of thirty or more children, each one different in ability and personality.

Teachers' understanding of parents

Every day thousands of parents watch with mingled pride and apprehension as their children go off to school—with pride because at school Johnny or Mary will learn the things which will equip them for useful citizenship; with apprehension lest their child may not adjust well to the school situation or learn as easily as the child next door.

Since this child is so important to them personally and since he spends nearly all his time either in his home or at school, it is essential that parent and teacher work closely together to provide the best possible conditions for his development. From kindergarten through high school, effective communication between teacher and parent, involving the sharing of information and cooperative planning, can do wonders to help Johnny or Mary adjust to circumstances which may be difficult for them. Just as an example, let's see how this worked out in the case of Bobby.

Bobby is a little fellow who, about a year ago, began to lash out at other children, biting, scratching, grabbing and destroying their possessions, and, in general, doing a great deal to upset the classroom. His last year's teacher had been unable to make progress with him in spite of a parent conference.

Miss Craig, Bobby's teacher for this year, has been working very hard with the little fellow but hasn't had much success either. We find her now mulling the problem over in her mind and finally having such thoughts as these: "I'm going to have to send for that child's parents, but I surely hate to. His last year's teacher said they were antagonistic and gave her no help at all. Well, I'll give it a try anyhow, but I'd better get Bobby's consent first."

"Bobby, I'll bet you'd like your Mommy to come down and see your room here and some of the things you've built at school, wouldn't you? She could see where you sit and what you have in your desk and that nice horse you drew yesterday. And maybe Mommy and I could figure out a way to help you be happier with the other boys and girls. Would you like that? O.K. I'll write Mommy a note and you can take it home to her tonight."

Dear Mrs. Miller:

As you may know, I have your little boy Bobby in my class this year. He's a fine little fellow and I'm very much interested in him. I'm most anxious to help him all I can and, somehow, I feel that if I could get acquainted with you so that we could share our information and make some plans together for him, I could work with him much better. Won't you come down to see me at your earliest convenience? I should be so happy to meet you.

Sincerely,

(Miss) Ann Craig

This teacher was wise to get the child's consent and to make his mother's visit a cooperative project with him. If a child, especially an adolescent, fears or resents having his parents sent for, the teacher may do more harm than good if she insists on seeing them against his will. She was wise, too, to use a friendly, positive approach in her letter. Let's see now how the parents reacted.

Mother to Father: Well! Here's another letter from the school. I just hate to open it. It will probably be like that one we got last year, telling us what a problem Bobby is and that we must come down and talk about it.

Father: *Well, why don't you open this letter? Maybe it hasn't anything to do with Bobby.*

Mother: *This is about Bobby, but it's a nice note from his new teacher. Do you suppose she just wants to get acquainted with me, or do you think maybe he has had some more difficulty?*

Father: *Well, whatever is behind it, she seems to be interested in our boy. Why don't you go over and see her tomorrow?*

Mother: *All right. I'll do that.*

What a natural reaction for this mother to have. A bungled conference with last year's teacher had made her hostile toward the school. Even though the friendly note from this year's teacher disarmed her considerably, she was still rather suspicious and really quite anxious. Let's see now how the interview with the new teacher went. We'll give you some excerpts from it.

We find Mrs. Miller entering Miss Craig's classroom almost immediately after school.

Mother: *I'm Mrs. Miller, Bobby's mother. I got your note and thought I'd come right over. Is Bobby in some kind of trouble?*

Teacher: *How do you do. Sit down, won't you? I'm so glad to meet Bobby's mother. Did you walk over?*

Mother: *Yes, it was such a beautiful day.*

Teacher: *Incidentally, Bobby brought some pretty leaves in to show the class yesterday. He seems to have quite an appreciation for pretty things.*

Mother: *Yes, he does seem to.*

Teacher: *His little friend Mary had a very pretty top which was all decorated with bright flowers. Bobby thought it was so pretty that he wanted it. And, sure enough, in just a minute he got it away from her. . . .*

Mother: *I've noticed that he does take things away from other children and is very rough with them. I don't quite know what to do about it.*

Teacher: *Perhaps he's a little impulsive. Tell me more about him. What is he like at home? Is he pretty active?*

Mother: *Oh, dear! Is he ever! He's into everything. And sometimes he's quite destructive.*

Teacher: *Are there any particular times when he's destructive—that is, is he likely to want to break something or grab something when he's displeased or when he's tired, or if he's scolded, or . . .*

Mother: *Well, he almost always gets naughty when the baby is brought into the room.*

Teacher: *Oh—yes, Bobby did tell me that he had a baby sister.*

Mother: *Yes, and he is jealous of her. But, my goodness, we can't keep her locked in a closet all the time. After all, she's a year old.*

Teacher: *Of course not! But maybe it has been hard on Bobby not to be the center of attention. He's such a loving little fellow that he probably figures he could use all of your affection and attention for himself.*

Mother: *Yes, I suppose he could. Do you think he needs a lot? More than other youngsters, I mean?*

Teacher: *All children that age need lots of attention, and, of course, they need it at some times more than at others. Right now Bobby seems to demand quite a bit at home and at school. Most of the time he's a pretty good little boy and he does quite well with his reading and arithmetic, but if I haven't been able to center my attention on him, he may run around the room or hit some other child or perhaps grab something on the desk here. But as soon as I put my arm around him and talk to him, he calms right down and gets back to his work.*

Mother: *He does seem to respond to affection. Maybe the baby has taken more time than I had realized. And maybe I haven't taken as much time with Bobby as I should—that is, in an affectionate sort of way. He gets into things so that I guess I'm nagging at him quite a bit. Perhaps my nagging at him and spending so much time with the baby make him feel that I don't care as much as I really do. I think maybe my husband should play with him more, too.*

Teacher: *That's a very good idea. Attention and affection are so necessary for all youngsters because it makes them feel secure and important. I'll give him as much as I can here, too. Perhaps all of us can show more interest in the things that Bobby feels are important. So often what we think is important is quite different from his ideas.*

Mother: *I hadn't thought about that, but it's true, isn't it? Well, we'll keep that in mind, too. I'm glad now that you got in touch with me.*

Teacher: *Well, I'm so glad you could take the time to come. You have an active, alert little boy, and you can be sure that I'm interested in everything concerning him. Won't you come back after a little while so that we can compare notes and see how much progress we're making?*

Mother: *Yes, I'll be glad to. This conference has really been helpful. It's wonderful to know that you are so interested in Bobby and are doing so much to help him. It makes me want to really do the things we've talked about. Thank you so much. Good-bye.*

This mother was basically an understanding and affectionate parent. That made communication easy. She was able to give and receive information about Bobby. The teacher's positive attitude toward the child helped to dispel the mother's initial antagonism toward the school. With the teacher's help, she was able to gain some insight into what seemed to be an underlying problem. Acting on the hypothesis that a desire for attention and affection might be at the bottom of Bobby's undesirable school and home behavior, mother, father, and teacher might supply this need in many little ways. Leaving the door open for further conferences would be an incentive to the mother to follow up on her present insights and good intentions.

Educators should remember that the parents' ego is inextricably tied up with their children. Their children are a major part of them—something which they have produced, something which represents what they are giving to society, something in which their hopes and dreams are all wrapped up. Our teacher, in the interview, realized all this. She spoke kindly of Bobby. She focused on his need for attention and affection rather than on his bad behavior in class.

Educators are prone to berate parents either for spoiling their children or for being too strict or too inconsistent or whatever makes the children problems in the classroom. This is a very natural thing to do, for when a teacher, for instance, is faced with thirty-five or forty children, several of whom are so-called "problem children" who practically ruin his class, he tends to blame someone for his difficulties. The parents are the natural objects. While he might rightfully blame them, however, he still must realize that the ways in which these parents handle their children stem from the way they themselves were brought up or from problems in the home situation, many of which are impossible for anyone to cope with. The teacher, then, while perhaps rightfully putting the blame in the home, still must be understanding of and sympathetic toward the parents. If he can do this, then he can enter into parent conferences with a kindly attitude of wanting to help. It is only with such an approach that a parent-teacher conference can be successful.

Parents' understanding of teachers

Parents are people. So are teachers. The great majority of teachers are in the school business because they like children and take satisfaction in seeing them develop. They take pride in their own school, too—in the philosophy they have helped to develop, in the methods and techniques they have acquired and used successfully, but, perhaps most of all, in what they do from day to day to help children to learn subject matter and ways to get along with people.

Because of their feelings about all these things, teachers have searched for the best possible ways to work successfully.

They want to help children and they want the public to have faith in them, as individuals, and in their methods of teaching. Through the years, they have found that knowing the parents, sharing information with them about the children, and talking to them frequently in a face-to-face relationship about the ways of the classroom, methods of teaching, and such, help to foster a fine feeling of mutual confidence which is of real ultimate value to the welfare of the child. Parents should and do appreciate teachers' genuine concern for their children.

Approaches to parents

The approach is important for effective communication. The teacher should focus the interview on what the parent wants to know; it should be parent-centered. For example, Mrs. Patten came to an interview concerned about her son's social adjustment in the fifth grade. In reply to her question, "How has Dan been?" the teacher said, "His work has been excellent except in arithmetic."

Mrs. P.: *I didn't mean his work. I mean how has he been? Does he like school?*

Teacher: *Frankly, no. That has bothered me. I thought you might have some explanation.*

Mrs. P.: *I'm afraid Dan isn't enjoying school very much. He seems to feel that you don't like him. He says you call others by their nicknames, but you always call him Daniel. I wish you'd call him Dan.*

Teacher: *Why, of course. You see, we use nicknames when we have more than one child with the same name. We have only the one Daniel, and so I called him by his full name, never realizing he felt this way about it.*

Mrs. P.: *Thank you. I wish he were more popular with the others. He seems to be friendly with only two boys in his class.*

Teacher: *I think I can help him along that line by our work in small groups. I noticed he knows a great deal about famous athletes. Through sports, he should become better acquainted with other boys.*

Mrs. P.: *Oh, he knows all about the ballplayers, but he lacks coordination. I wish he could spend some time at sports. He's so awkward.*

Teacher: *I'm in charge of an afternoon sports program for boys in grades five and six, but I've seen Dan in the group only once.*

Mrs. P.: *That was because he was the last one chosen and he feels that none of the boys wants him on their team.*

Teacher: *I think we can avoid that problem in the future.*

Mrs. P.: *That would be good. . . .*

Teacher: *He can read much better than most of the other children, but I'd like to do some work with him after school in arithmetic. He is falling behind his group, and I'd rather try to pull him up than shift him to another group. Would you mind if I asked him to stay after school a short while two afternoons next week?*

Mrs. P.: *Not at all. Will he be able to make the second bus trip home?*

Teacher: *I'll see that he does. Now, are there any other ways in which you think I might help him?*

Mrs. P.: *Yes, I'd like to see his handwriting improved. He just scratches and clings like mad to his pencil.*

Teacher: *I think he was doing manuscript writing when he came here. We start cursive writing in the fourth grade; so he missed the change-over process. We have a handwriting specialist in the school system, and I'll speak to her about Dan. She will tell me about any special exercises or instruction he may need.*

Mrs. P.: *Thank you very much. That should be just the help he needs. He tells me he doesn't like to write stories, but likes to tell them. If his writing improves, I'm sure he'll enjoy writing stories as well.*

Teacher: *His poor writing may also be related to his trouble in arithmetic. I've required him to hand in carefully written papers.*

Mrs. P.: *He told me you made him do his papers over several times because they were not neat enough. . . .*

Teacher: *You've been a great help to me, Mrs. Patten. Now I think I can be of more help to Dan.*

Mrs. P.: *And I think we've covered all the things I wanted to speak about. Are there any questions I could answer?*

Teacher: *No, I don't think there is anything else now, but I hope to see you before too long so that we may compare notes about Dan's progress.*

Mrs. P.: *I'll drop in to see you in three or four weeks.*

In this ten-minute interview, the teacher, who felt that the main problem was Dan's poor work in arithmetic, first gave his attention to the mother's concern about her son's social adjustment and suggested ways in which he might help. It was after considering this matter that he asked about the possibility of keeping Dan after school for extra help in arithmetic. The arithmetic and the handwriting, which Mrs. Patten mentioned later, were also of concern to her.

Mrs. Patten left the conference with a feeling of satisfaction because, as she said, "We've covered all the things I wanted to speak about," and because the teacher had tried to find some concrete solution for each problem. Apparently the teacher was genuinely interested in Dan; this interview seems to have given him specific insights into Dan's sensitivity in social situations and paved the way for improvement in arithmetic.

In our next interview, the parent was a father who would not allow his son Henry, a sophomore in high school, to come out for basketball. Henry had no friends, was tall and shy and retiring, and was doing poor academic work. The father began the interview by saying, "I suppose you've come to get my permission to have Henry play on the basketball team."

Teacher (who was also the athletic coach): *Yes, I'd like that very much.*

Mr. C. (in a bitter tone): *Well, my answer is still no! I need Henry here at home after school to help me. He's the only boy I have left after Frank went in the Army. Why don't people let other people alone? I don't approve of all the school parties and athletics. If we would all keep our children at home and tend to our own business, it would be better. That's why I tell my children—"Don't bother with anyone else and you'll not get into trouble."*

Teacher: *You have very well-behaved children, Mr. C. All the teachers feel the same way about them. But I have the feeling Henry needs the interest in athletics.*

Mr. C.: *Oh, he gets enough exercise around here on the farm. If he weren't so lazy! You've got to keep after that boy all the time to get him to do anything.*

Teacher: *There may be some truth in the old saying, "All work and no play makes Jack a dull boy."*

Mr. C.: *You mean . . .*

Teacher: *Yes, Henry might work better at home and at school if he had more fun in his life and more success in something he can do well. But he'll not go out for basketball unless he has your approval.*

Mr. C.: *Well, I can't be going into town to pick him up after practice and after games.*

Teacher: *We can take care of the transportation problem.*

Mr. C.: *Thanks, but I still have to get my work done around the farm.*

Teacher: *Perhaps Henry would work harder and more willingly if he got pleasure from being on the team. Why don't you give it a try, Mr. C.? I think Henry would make as fine a basketball player as his cousin Francis, who won an athletic scholarship to college.*

Mr. C. (smiling): *Do you really think so?*

Teacher: *Yes, I do.*

Mr. C.: *Let me think it over.*

Teacher: *Please do, and thanks for taking the time to talk about it.*

The following Monday, Henry came out for basketball. Two months later Mr. C. and his family came to the stadium and watched Henry play an outstanding game. After the game Mr. C. said to the teacher, "I've been wanting to talk with you the past week or so. I want to thank you for all you've done for Henry. He certainly has changed since I gave him permission to play basketball. He works harder on the farm and takes more responsibility. I don't have to prod him much any more."

Teacher: *That's fine, Mr. C. His schoolwork has improved, too. You'll see improvement on his next report card, I'm sure.*

Mr. C.: *Tonight was the first time I ever saw Henry play. It certainly made me feel proud to hear all those people cheering for him.*

Teacher: *You've got a fine boy, Mr. C., and you have a right to be proud of him.*

In his first interview with Mr. C., the teacher, while recognizing the father's point of view, pushed him into deciding to let Henry play. This procedure seemed to be justified by its immediate results. However, the father did not permit Henry to go out for baseball in the spring. This negative decision had an adverse effect on the boy's attitude and academic work.

To be most effective, a conference should give a parent the opportunity to discuss whatever is uppermost in his mind about the child. In presenting information, the teacher should bear in mind the parent's point of view. Teachers sometimes conduct a conference as though the parent were not a person in his own right but merely an obstruction to be got around—for the child's good, of course. Teachers should be aware that parents have feelings and attitudes that are the product of a certain background, which may be more or less revealed by their remarks about themselves and their child.

Parents vary widely in their receptivity to information and to new points of view. Some irritably resist any change, while others accept almost anything with the greatest docility. Midway between these two extremes is the ability and willingness to weigh evidence before accepting or rejecting it—the ability to arrive at one's own decisions.

Having facts to communicate

Parent-teacher conferences often fail because the teacher does not know enough about the child. Parents want accurate information. As one mother said, "I didn't make the effort to come to the school and hire a baby-sitter just to hear that Jane was a very nice child."

The teacher should have a folder for each child, containing dated samples of his work, anecdotal records that can be periodically summarized, and a well-kept cumulative record. All these enable the teacher to supply and interpret facts about the child that will be helpful to the parent.

Nonverbal communication

Communication is not necessarily verbal. A teacher may betray a feeling of inferiority by a subdued voice, a sagging posture, downcast eyes, hesitant speech, and many other expressive signs. He may express antagonism toward a parent by a brusque manner, a grim facial expression, and movements that indicate impatience. One shows genuine regard for another person by giving him close attention, smiling in encouragement or approval, and considering his physical comfort. The language of behavior is extensive and subtle. The skilled interviewer is aware of the importance of such nonverbal communication. It is the most effective way of showing a parent that he cares.

Verbal communication

There are many ways in which verbal communication may affect
the success of the parent-teacher conference. It often happens
that parents and teachers do not speak the same language; they
are separated by seas of misunderstanding. Thus what the teacher
says does not evoke the desired response from the parent. Mis-
understandings may also arise when the teacher speaks too rapidly, uses long, involved sentences, or fails to cite concrete
examples. Sometimes the teacher is too impersonal; the conference degenerates into a lecture on education.

But parent-teacher conferences require two-way communication; what we have said about the teacher's ability to convey
facts and feeling applies also to the parent.

Speaking their language

Words that are the least bit abstract are likely to be misinterpreted. Meanings are derived from experiences, and no two
people have had the same experiences. For example, Stuart Chase
obtained a different definition of communism from every person
he asked to define it.

Moreover, each professional group has its own jargon. Before
we know it, we teachers tend to lapse into pedagese. Thus our
interviews sometimes sound like this:

"Your boy needs association and companionship for personality development and emotional stability."

"By engaging in athletics, your boy is more likely to become
recognized and accepted by his peer group. At present he is very
much of an extrovert."

"How do you think your child is adjusting to school?"

Ideas of this kind can be stated in lay language:

"There are times when 'a feller needs a friend.' Playing on
a team is a good way to make friends and learn to get along well
with different kinds of people."

"How does your child like school? Do you think of anything we can do to help him get along well in school?"

Good communication is clear communication. It will not be clear if each person, because of his different background, interprets the words differently or if, as in *Alice in Wonderland,* each person makes a word mean what he chooses it to mean.

The more we listen to what the other person wants to tell us, the likelier we are to avoid this danger. If we give him a chance to present himself and his problem in his own way, we gain enough understanding to communicate with him. It is when we begin to be didactic that we lose connection with him.

Being simple and concrete   *but not too general.*

Simple sentences are easier to grasp, in both listening and reading. In listening, especially, it is difficult to keep modifying phrases and clauses in mind. Plain talk is best. We have known persons whose sentences were so long and intricate, or so ill-organized, that we lost track of what they were talking about by the time they came to the end of the sentence.

Disjointed sentences are hard to grasp. A birdbrain flits from one idea to another, and the second may be totally unrelated to the first. What this person says never adds up to anything definite. On the other hand, it is easy to follow the thought in a logical succession of sentences.

Some people, like the nurse in *Romeo and Juliet,* are afflicted with total recall. Their wordiness is wearisome. They are like the man who, when asked the time of day, builds a watch for you. Only an astute listener can separate the few grains of wheat from the bushels of chaff. Parent-teacher conferences are not long enough to permit a high percentage of irrelevant conversation.

Perhaps the teacher's most common fault in parent conferences is being too general. A parent conference that consists only of generalizations gives the parent nothing concrete to take hold of. To be meaningful, a generalization must be built on a solid foundation of concrete facts. To tell a parent his child is doing poorly in school is of even less help than the traditional report card that gives letter grades in each subject. The parent needs to know what the child's specific difficulties are, what is causing them, and what he can do to help the child overcome them.

Conversation that is direct, specific, simple, and concrete is most likely to convey the ideas intended. It is most likely to move the parent to action.

Speaking effectively

The way in which words are said may enhance or diminish their effect. If we mumble or speak too rapidly, even our best ideas are lost. Our tone of voice may suggest a desire to dominate, which may be resented; or uncertainty, which may create doubt in the mind of the listener; or a positive conviction, which inspires confidence. A regional accent may alienate one from people whose speech is different. Two teachers from the North were referred to as "furriners" in a Southern community. This kind of difference not only interferes with comprehension, but also tends to prevent one from being fully accepted by the community as "one of us."

The element of feeling that is conveyed by words should not be neglected. One word that has an emotional connotation may make or mar the rapport between teacher and parent. Sometimes teachers unknowingly use words that are emotionally loaded in a particular community.

Personalizing communication

A parent-teacher conference is more useful in establishing good relationships between parents and teachers than in imparting information. Information can be given in other ways. The conference is the best way of developing mutual respect and appreciation. The teacher should show consideration for the convenience and comfort of the parent; this is an obvious way of promoting good feeling. More fundamentally, he should recognize and accept the parent's feelings, whether they are hostile or friendly, discouraged or hopeful.

As the conversation proceeds, the alert teacher will pick up clues and follow up on them. For example, if a parent says, "My child is exceptionally shy," the teacher may ask, "Just how does he show his shyness?" Parents appreciate a teacher who shows sympathy and concern for their troubles. For example, after a mother had described the trouble her son caused her and had spoken of the grandparent's interference with her management of the child, the teacher said sympathetically, "That must have been very difficult for you." At the end of the interview, she said reassuringly, "You have helped already by talking it over with me."

Both parent and teacher should leave the interview with a feeling of satisfaction—with the conviction that "it was good for us to have been here." Both should have obtained some insight into the child's best development, his behavior, or some clarification of a specific problem; they should have reached some specific decision about the next step to be taken or should have made a positive change in their perception of the child or of themselves. The true test of the success of a parent-teacher conference is to be found in the parent's subsequent behavior toward the child and the effect this has on him.

Parent education

Parents are educators. Historically, before schools were built,
the education of children was their responsibility. Today parents
still hold this position of responsibility for the education of young
children. During school years, the parents' role as teacher is
diminished, but it by no means disappears.

Overview of parent education

Some parents are excellent teachers. They seem to know intuitively ways to facilitate children's learning. A large majority of
parents, however, need guidance in bringing up their children.
They need preparation for their job, just as teachers do. The
late James S. Plant once said that much of our child guidance
should become parent guidance.

Parents are influenced in many ways. Relatives and friends
give gratuitous and often misleading advice. Pediatricians today
are concerned with all aspects of the child's development throughout the periods of infancy and early childhood. Dr. Spock has
spoken to thousands of parents through his books. Newspaper

columns and magazine articles, public health and social work agencies, churches, and other organizations are concerned with the child in the family.

Parent education is becoming increasingly important. Every school system has the obligation to integrate the education that goes on in the school with education in the home. Parents and teachers *are* partners. They need to learn how to work together.

The parent education program includes notes and leaflets sent home; evaluation of radio and TV programs; school visits; PTA and other meetings; study groups; classes in child development, such as "How to help your child succeed in school," as well as in art, music, drama, handicrafts, and other subjects that contribute to the personal development and happiness of parents as persons. Parent-teacher conferences and home visits are the most personalized and, in many ways, the most important part of the total parent education program.

Guiding principles and procedures in parent education include the following assumptions:

Parents want the best for their children; they do not want to be "problem parents."

They can often change their behavior or redirect it in beneficial ways, even though they cannot change their basic personality.

Like other people, they need acceptance and approval. Blaming the parents gets nowhere fast.

Parent education should start where the parents are and proceed wisely and slowly from there.

Parents can help teachers as much as teachers can help parents; parent education is a two-way service as well as two-way communication.

Parents usually want honest, up-to-date, accurate information, not platitudes and vague generalizations.

Parents are often relieved and helped by hearing how other parents have handled problems similar to theirs.

Parent education materials and procedures

Printed materials

There is a vast amount of reading material directed to parents. Numerous books deal with the parents' responsibility for the education of gifted children or of slow learners, with delinquency and creativity, with success in reading and other school subjects, with preparing for and entering college—in short, with every important aspect of child and adolescent development. Pamphlets for parents are even more numerous. Books or pamphlets may be recommended by the teacher in a parent-teacher conference. Recommendation of printed material is one of the most effective ways to further the parent's understanding of some question that has been raised in an interview.

The Department of Elementary School Principals in conjunction with the National School Public Relations Association (National Education Association, Washington 6, D.C.) and the National Congress of Parents and Teachers has published a 32-page pamphlet called *Happy Journey, Preparing Your Child for School*. This is a handbook for parents whose children will soon enter kindergarten or first grade. It is concrete and practical, amusingly illustrated, and well stocked with answers to many of the questions that parents ask. Another pamphlet deals with speech development—*Helping Children Talk Better* by C. van Riper. This is published by Science Research Associates, Inc., in Chicago, Illinois. It discusses the development of speech sounds, the child's first attempts to say words, speech defects, and the importance of learning to listen as well as talk. The area of reading is considered from the parents' standpoint in Paul Witty's Science Research Associates pamphlet, *Helping Children Read Better*. One chapter is devoted to preschool prereading experiences; other chapters deal with reading in the subsequent school years. Another excellent pamphlet for the parent whose child will soon be learning to read is *Janie Learns to Read*; it may be ordered from the Department of Elementary School Principals or the National School Public Relations Association, Washington 6, D.C. This pamphlet describes the specific kinds of preschool experiences that prepare the child for beginning reading in school. It is most readable and attractively illustrated. (A librarian should be consulted for details on procuring the materials mentioned.)

Many school systems have published similar pamphlets for parents of preschool children. Any of these materials will also give teachers of older children an excellent background for their parent conferences about preschool years.

There is also a wealth of articles in local and national newspapers and magazines; in educational magazines, newspapers, and bulletins; and in the mimeographed letters and bulletins that are sent out by local schools or school systems. One school distributed an effective letter in which one parent gave other parents perceptive, accurate, and reassuring information about reading.

Parent-teacher conferences are a fertile source of ideas for preparing many kinds of written material. In conferences parents reveal their points of view and show their concern about certain problems. Parents and teachers often arrive at original solutions which are sound and should be shared with others.

How effective printed parent education material is no one knows exactly. We surmise that it is most effective when it has a personal appeal; is relevant to the parents' present interest; deals with a problem the parent can do something about; is written in a readable, stimulating style; and is recommended by someone in whom the parent has confidence. The extent to which printed material is accepted and used will vary with the interests, needs, and cultural traditions of the parents to whom it is given.

In recommending printed material, the teacher should have some knowledge of the reading ability of the parents and the reading difficulty of the material. The majority of the state and national pamphlets that were analyzed in one study were at the seventh- or eighth-grade level of reading difficulty. Many parents of public school children have trouble reading sixth-grade books.

Books and pamphlets may provide parents with a store of common knowledge. With this as a base, it is easier to go further in the discussion of an individual child.

Radio and television programs

Some radio and television programs are more helpful than others. Some do more harm than good by heightening parental anxieties and doubts. Some are far too prescriptive; they give rigid rules without regard for individual differences in parents, children, and home conditions. Other programs are misleading in their total impact, even though their component statements may be accurate. Television stations too often present educational programs without checking the competency of the educators who are responsible for them. A few are skillfully planned and presented with fidelity and finesse. To make sure that parent education programs are both accurate and effective, a specialist in preparing materials for the mass media should team up with an expert in child development and parent education.

In the parent-teacher conference, the teacher may mention the best current programs and give the parent some criterion for judging this type of offering. Some parents also need to be warned against misleading commercials.

Although emotional appeals may get certain immediate results, they are less desirable in the long run than a rational approach that helps parents become more independent and competent in making their own decisions.

When a parent is motivated and receptive to suggestions, a positive approach is much better than one that arouses fear or anxiety. The detrimental effects of a frightening or otherwise negative approach usually outweigh any shock value that it may have.

A comparative evaluation of various mass-media programs might well be considered in parent-teacher conferences. We have already mentioned the need for clarity in communication. The effective parent-teacher conference is also marked by a rational rather than an emotional appeal and a positive rather than a negative approach.

Group meetings

Much information can be given parents in groups by demonstrations, recordings, films, lectures, and discussions. Thus conference time is saved for more specific applications to the individual child. Group meetings give the school people a chance to interpret school methods and procedures, course content, and the like. Modern schools have been repeatedly criticized because their methods differ from those used when the present generation of parents were in school. We know, for instance, that children learn to read more efficiently under present methods than under former ones, but the public isn't convinced because we haven't taken the time to interpret the methods and how they operate. The public cries for the good old use of phonics. Naturally. But we haven't taken the time to explain to parents that we still teach phonics, only in a more meaningful way.

The public wants to be sure that we are teaching history and wonders what in the world social studies and social living are all about. We need to let them know that their children are getting as much history in social studies and social living classes as children have ever got—again in a more meaningful way. Teachers and administrators should take every opportunity to interpret the school program. Individual conferences are particularly effective with critical parents.

Group meetings may take many forms (see Chapter 3). According to research studies, lectures seem to be generally less effective than group discussions; and when led by an expert in the field, group discussions have been found to be more effective than when led by a layman. However, fairly good results have been obtained by use of a team comprised of a lay leader trained in discussion methods and an expert in the content.

Panels of teachers and parents have been used to initiate general discussion of a topic. Under skillful leadership, panels of children and young people have aroused keen interest by the views they frankly and directly express.

Meetings in which a teacher demonstrates a teaching method with a group of children are always popular. More and more films, slide films, and recordings are being used as springboards for discussion.

Programs are more likely to meet the needs of the group if they are planned by the members than if they are planned by people who are unfamiliar with their immediate concerns.

Child-study groups, such as those developed by Daniel Prescott, have been helpful to parents as well as to teachers. The first-year program in these groups consists of intensive study of individual children—collecting information about the child, interpreting it, and testing the hypotheses suggested.

Many methods are combined in the workshop type of program: lectures, films, recordings, and various forms of group discussion. One careful evaluation of this type of program showed that the parents who participated made significant gains in knowledge. Changes in parents' attitudes and behavior and in their children's attitudes and behavior are the most important outcomes of parent education; these are seldom accurately measured.

Discussion-group therapy is group-centered and conducted in a highly permissive atmosphere. Members of the group are encouraged to express their thoughts and feelings. They help one another by discussing common problems and describing ways of handling them that have or have not worked. It requires skilled leadership to keep the interaction in the group as beneficial as possible to all the members. In the course of sessions of this type, many changes have been noted in parents' expressed attitudes. Whether these have been translated into actual changes in their attitudes and behavior toward their children is more difficult to ascertain.

Opportunities for observation

To acquaint parents with the school's program and methods of teaching, it is effective to give them opportunities to observe, as in a parent-night program, an open-school week, or unscheduled visits to their child's classroom. In some parent-night programs, the parents go through a telescoped school day; they go from class to class as their children do, but for shorter periods. In each class the teacher shows samples of the children's work and demonstrates or explains the methods she is using. During open-school week, parents may visit any classes and stay as long as they wish. Children serve as hostesses and guides. These visits are more valuable if parents receive later some explanation of the procedures they have observed. This can sometimes be made most effectively when parents visit the child's classroom at their convenience during the school year and stay until the teacher has a few free minutes to talk with them.

Reporting pupil progress

The purpose of reports of student progress is to enable parents to help their children make a better school record. Any type of report is to be judged by its contribution to this purpose.

What effect does the traditional report card actually have? It causes great anxiety on the part of some children. They are afraid to take it home. They even think about running away from home. Not knowing how to do better, they have no constructive outlet for their fears. Others try to escape punishment or loss of privileges by promising to work harder. In a few days, however, their resolution wavers, and they settle back into their old indolent routine. Still others, who are very fond of their parents, are unhappy to have disappointed them. A few happy-go-lucky youngsters seem, on the surface at least, to be unperturbed by a poor report card. It has no effect on their achievement. Those who receive high grades and complimentary comments are sometimes so elated that they cannot resist flaunting their superiority. The child who fails or makes low grades in order to get even with his parents for one reason or another gains a certain sense of satisfaction from bringing home a poor report.

On the whole, the traditional type of report is of little help to either parent or child. Parents learn that the child is doing superior, average, or below-average work according to grade standard, but they do not know why, or how he can improve.

Other forms of reporting are somewhat better. A report card that includes a comment on the grades or an explanation of them may give the child a toe hold to start climbing upward. A letter to the parents may be still more helpful. It has been found, however, that such letters tend to become stereotyped, polite rather than frank, and vague rather than specific, and that they are burdensome to the teacher.

The report that takes the form of a check list comprising a large number of specific items is easier for the teacher to fill out; however, he is tempted to check items on which he has an inadequate basis of observation. Moreover, such a check list does not show the central importance of certain items and their relation to other aspects of the child's development.

It is more helpful to set up an accurate analysis of the various types of knowledge and skill that are necessary in each subject. Proficiency in each of these can be rated by both pupil and teacher. This kind of report shows parent and child where the child needs help. For example, in science he may be good in setting up experiments but weak in his knowledge of technical words.

To give parents some indication as to whether a child is working up to his capacity, a few schools have developed a dual marking system. One mark shows his achievement in relation to that of others of his age and grade; the other mark indicates his achievement in relation to his ability as far as that can be determined. Thus a slow-learning child might get a mark of C in relation to grade standards and an A in relation to his capacity to achieve. The great trouble with this system is that capacity is difficult to evaluate. Group tests of intelligence are misleading, especially in the case of poor readers, emotionally disturbed children, and those with foreign-language backgrounds who do not speak English fluently.

Any modification in the reporting system should be worked out cooperatively; it should not be imposed suddenly upon parents and teachers. It will be successful only if it is understood and accepted by all concerned.

Parent-teacher conferences

Of all the methods of parent education, the one that offers the best opportunity to interpret a child's school record and do something to help him improve it is the parent-teacher conference. Such conferences are held in the majority of schools today and are considered one of the modern teacher's responsibilities. In schools where they have been held, parents and teachers have expressed much satisfaction with them.

There are many reasons for parent-teacher interviews, but they all add up to: "The child shall benefit."

Reasons for conferences

Let us consider, now, some specific instances wherein a teacher-parent interview will ultimately benefit the child.

Perhaps one of the most important reasons for a parent-teacher interview is to give the teacher the opportunity to supplement the written reports of progress. There is a general trend throughout the country for such conferences, either to replace the old report card or at least to add to it immeasurably. Written reports of progress, at best, tell very little about the child. He can be rated by grades or by check marks or whatever, but how objectively is he being measured and by whose standards and in competition with whom—his classmates, others whom the teacher has taught before, or himself? Even when space for comments is provided, teachers find it difficult to tell the whole story.

Supplementary conferences, then, are indeed important if the parents are to get a helpful picture of the development of the child, which they can do something about.

Parents *want to know* how well or how poorly their child is doing in school. They have a right and a responsibility to know. How many parents have you heard berating the elementary schools when their child, who they thought had been getting along nicely, comes home from junior high school with poor grades and comments on the report card to the effect that he is lacking in the fundamentals? And how many disturbed parents have you met who had supposed their child was doing quite all right in junior high school, according to grades received, only to find that he was unable to make decent grades in senior high school? And so it goes all the way up to college. So parents do need to have an honest evaluation of their child as he moves along from one level to the next. Face-to-face conferences are the most effective ways for teachers to impart this information.

Administrators consider parent-teacher conferences important for public relations. Parents thus get acquainted with the teachers and the school. In most instances, they both express satisfaction in the interviews they have had.

Kinds of conferences

As was indicated earlier, parent conferences can be most beneficial when a child presents a problem, whether a behavior problem or a problem having to do with underachievement. The sharing of information and an understanding of a common problem can help immeasurably to give both teacher and parent insights into what might well be the best approach to a solution. Plans made together wherein each person has specific ideas to carry out and certain responsibilities to take can make a tremendous difference in a child's life. Sharing and planning together are good psychologically, too, for both the parent and the teacher. The very thought of knowing that someone else is sharing in this responsibility—that another person is vitally interested in this child with a problem—helps each one to move along with a little more confidence and a little more faith.

Many times parents are too ambitious for their children, expecting far more of them than the youngsters are able to produce. These children become most unhappy and many times so tense that they cannot begin to work even up to the capacity they have. Most certainly a conference is in order at a time like this. This is, perhaps, one of the most difficult kinds to conduct. As has been mentioned before, the ego of the parents is very definitely involved with their child. Therefore they are most anxious about the success of their child. The child is so much a part of them. If he succeeds, they feel like successful parents and take pride in all his accomplishments. If he fails, they feel that they, too, have failed in some way.

It is not easy, then, for a teacher or an educator to sit down with a parent and attempt to help him understand that his child is not a superior student, that he is just average, and that no amount of pressure will make him produce that of which he is not capable. Perhaps reading the recording of actual interviews of this type of conference will help the reader to get a sense of how to approach the problem.

Of course, still more difficult is the conference with the parent of a mentally retarded youngster, that is, a youngster whose IQ falls under 70. Here again, the parents' ego is highly involved. Often these parents labor with feelings of guilt, thinking that somehow they have been to blame for the predicament of the child. It is extremely difficult for parents to accept the fact that their child is retarded and that placement in a special type of class is the best thing for him, and it takes real skill on the part of the educator to help them. Ordinarily, psychologists handle such conferences. An illustrative interview conducted by a psychologist is presented in Chapter 10.

On the other end of the scale, we find a happier kind of conference. This is with parents of the gifted. It is always a joy to be able to tell parents that they have a child with very outstanding ability; yet there are many cautions to be observed at such times. First of all, parents probably should not be told that their child *is* very superior but rather that he has great potential and great responsibilities. Parents need to know that, while intelligence is a very important factor in a child's life, there are other factors of equal importance, such as learning to get along with other people. They need to know, too, that conditions must be right for their child to realize the potential he possesses. These conditions are a joint responsibility of the home and school, and it is for this reason that the parent-teacher conference is so important. The reader may be interested in reading recorded interviews of such conferences in Chapter 9.

Time for conferences

It is all very well to talk about the importance of parent-teacher conferences and to note the kinds of conferences and the reasons for them, but where in the world can time be found for conducting them when teachers are already too busy, and how can teachers gain the skills necessary to make such conferences successful? This is indeed a good question. Many schools have recognized the importance of working out a solution to this problem and have tried various ways to approach it. Conferences should be scheduled during the school day if possible, but for parents who are at work during the day, they may be held in the evening hours. Some problems of scheduling are discussed in Chapter 4.

Need for in-service education

Teachers need in-service education for this responsibility. Most helpful is a practical workshop which covers the purpose of parent-teacher conferences, various types of conferences, methods of conducting them, and parental attitudes and expectations with respect to them.

In one school system, administrators, teachers, and parents spent a year studying the parent-teacher conference. Both parents and teachers filled out carefully constructed questionnaires, or "reactionnaires," in which they appraised the parent-teacher conferences with which they had had firsthand experience, under such headings as time, duration, content, method, and results. These reports were tabulated and summarized with the help of parents, and the recommendations that resulted from the study were carried out. Two major recommendations were (1) that there be an analysis of specific goals for each subject and that progress toward these goals be appraised at the end of each marking period by pupils and teachers jointly; and (2) that parent-teacher conferences on each pupil be held twice a year.

Evaluation of parent education

How effective is parent education? Can parents' attitudes be changed? Do parents follow the advice they receive? Do they apply the insights and suggestions that they gain from reading, listening to lectures, participating in parent-teacher conferences or other kinds of parent education?

Research on the evaluation of different kinds of parent education programs has been carefully reviewed by Brim.[1] Desirable changes in children constitute the best proof of the effectiveness of parent education. As parents acquire knowledge, they change their attitudes or their behavior toward the child. The child, in turn, changes his attitudes and behavior.

The content of group or individual programs and the methods by which parental attitudes are changed have been too poorly described to permit of any very helpful evaluation. Moreover, any method or content would have different effects on different kinds of parents.

From his studies of the effect of parent education, Brim concluded (1) that "parent education has had some measurable effects on the American parent"[2] and (2) that these effects are the result of long-term programs.

[1] Orville G. Brim, Jr., *Education for Child Rearing*, New York, Russell Sage Foundation, 1959. Chap. 9.
[2] *Ibid.*, p. 290.

However, the results of research on various methods and materials used in parent education are inconclusive. Some investigators report that group discussions have produced desirable changes in parental attitudes; others report no such changes. Similarly inconclusive results were obtained in the case of programs that used mass media and programs that used individual counseling. From these reports of research, one may draw either of two conclusions: (1) that adult attitudes and behavior are not changed by the kinds of parent education thus far attempted or (2) that while the changes produced by any one method are too small to be measured at any one time, they may in the long run constitute an important influence as parents are given a variety of educational experiences.

In addition to the evaluations we have mentioned, there is also a theoretical one—an evaluation of current programs of parent education in the light of sound educational theory. Each parent-teacher conference offers opportunity for evaluation.

Concluding statement

Different patterns of parent education are appropriate in different situations. With parents of high socioeconomic status, more reliance may be placed on printed material and an analytical type of report card. Such parents also welcome the opportunity to visit the school and talk with the teacher. They have a high regard for education, although they may be critical of present school practices. On the other hand, many parents who have little schooling themselves cannot understand either the written communications from the school or the books and pamphlets that are written for parents. They learn more from observation and personal contact with the teacher; if necessary, the teacher may use a student as an interpreter. Parent-teacher conferences help to clarify misconceptions, encourage parents to make and carry out decisions, and establish or maintain friendly relations between the home and the school.

Group meetings
with parents

CHAPTER THREE

*Guideposts to effective group meetings   Examples of group meetings
A team presentation   A room mothers' meeting   Specialists participate
as consultants*

Every teacher has meetings with parent groups. These are often
frightening, partly because teachers, like many other people, find
it difficult to talk to groups. Then, in addition to that, the teacher
may easily feel on the spot when faced with a large number of
parents of the children for whose development she has great
responsibility. She knows, too, that she must do a good job of
public relations. Almost always it is her job to interpret the
activities that go on in the classroom, and she knows how important it is for the parents to understand the kind of education
that she is attempting to give.

Guideposts to effective group meetings

Quite often the teacher is called upon to participate on a panel
with other members of the staff, such as the counselor and the
administrator and other teachers. Whatever the plan for talking
with groups of parents, there are a number of things which
should be kept in mind. Let us review some of these before we
get into any specific type of group meeting.

FIRST   The parents are interested in the teachers, as personalities, and so a teacher should make every effort to be well groomed and to establish an informal, friendly atmosphere. A humorous story often helps make the group initially receptive. The very nervous teacher might just remark that it always seems amusing to her that she, an old maid (if she is), has the nerve to come before a group of parents to tell them about their youngsters. This usually gets a sympathetic response from the parents because many of them do resent single teachers giving them a lot of theory out of books and taking the attitude of knowing more than the parents about their babes.

SECOND   Parents are eager to learn about the school program and will usually be friendly toward it if they are given an honest picture of it. Parents aren't fooled by a rosy picture which glosses over defects in the program. They need to know about the good things that are happening, to be sure, but they should also know about the difficulties which keep the program from being as effective as it should be. Many times their aid can be enlisted to correct some of the defects. On the whole, parents are sympathetic to the problems that teachers encounter and are glad to help in any way they can.

THIRD   Parents hate to be talked down to. Teachers, working with children all day, sometimes forget that in these meetings they are not still talking to children; consequently they have a manner of talking that is most distasteful to the audience. It's quite possible that many of the parents are as well educated and just as much on their toes as the teacher.

FOURTH   It is equally important for the teacher not to use the horrible pedagese of some educators and to talk in a way that is meaningless to a lay audience. The educator must remember that things which are very familiar to him may be completely unfamiliar to the parents. It is important for the teacher to be sure the parents are oriented to the thing she is talking about. The trick is to strike a balance between talking down to and talking over the heads of the audience. This can be accomplished if the teacher, in planning her talk, puts herself in the place of the average parent and somehow conveys a warm feeling.

FIFTH   The teacher should use many specific examples in interpreting the program and should have many of the instructional materials at hand to illustrate the points made. Generalities about any part of the program are seldom helpful and often can be grossly misinterpreted. To show exactly how reading is taught, some teachers have actually had a reading circle made up of parents from the audience and have gone through the process of a short reading lesson. Others have used a blackboard or other materials to explain the kind of thing they do. Still others have had some of the children come into a reading group and have given a ten-minute reading demonstration. In one school system, the reading consultant made short recordings of instruction in phonics in the first six grades. These recordings were played and discussed in the parents' meeting. There are various ways to show specifics, but shown they must be, and the clever teacher will find a good way.

SIXTH   It is wise to plan for as much parent participation as possible. Sometimes, before the conference, they can be asked to formulate questions they want answered. In organizing her remarks on the basis of the questions, the teacher has two advantages: (1) she includes the parent in the planning and (2) she has a chance to think through the answers and is likely to do a better job than if caught off guard with spontaneous questions at the time of the meeting. However, the speaker should always honor and deal with spontaneous questions. Good audience participation usually indicates a high interest in what's going on.

SEVENTH   There are many, many things which are of common interest to all parents and which will pertain specifically to their own child. These should be capitalized upon because each parent is particularly interested in the thing that is close to his own child.

EIGHTH   Some arrangement should be made so that the

teacher in elementary school can have at least a minute or two for each parent individually. Every parent likes to ask a question about his child or to tell the teacher something about him. It gives the whole thing a more personal touch.

NINTH   Teachers must be very careful in their remarks to say nothing that can be construed as being aimed at a particular child. No parent should be made to feel the least bit embarrassed or self-conscious.

TENTH   Teachers must remember that parents do not usually know about the special services a school system offers and that they will be very much interested in such information. It usually makes the parents feel proud of their school system when they learn of the many advantages offered in it.

ELEVENTH   Teachers should, if they honestly can, give the parents the feeling that they themselves are proud to be associated with the schools in that community. This tends to give the parents confidence in the schools, too. Confidence and pride make for good feeling.

TWELFTH   The teacher should always give the parents the feeling that they, the parents, with all the support they have given, are responsible for the opportunities provided for their children.

THIRTEENTH   Humor, kindliness, friendliness, and informality should pervade the whole meeting. The parents should be made to feel that the teacher is their friend and a friend of their children, that the schools belong to everyone, and that both parents and teachers are a working team whose main efforts are bent toward the welfare of the children.

Examples of group meetings

All these things and many more help to make for successful and fruitful group meetings with parents. Perhaps three or four examples of such meetings might be of help to teachers who are called upon to plan or participate in them.

A *team presentation*

In one elementary school, the teacher thought it would be interesting for the third-grade mothers to know in what ways the school staff worked with children. She, together with the principal, had already held two grade-level meetings in which they had made a real effort to explain the academic part of the program. These meetings had been highly successful. Now it seemed wise to follow up with another phase of the program. In the previous meetings the teacher had brought in the guidance done in the regular teaching process, but feeling that this might be done more specifically, she and the principal invited the supervisor of the city guidance program and the school counselor to participate in a panel in which all three would discuss the ways they worked with children. The supervisor was asked to chair the panel. Following is an outline of the way the panel operated:

The supervisor, who was quite an informal person, told a couple of appropriate humorous stories. These, together with complimentary remarks about the particular staff in that school and brief introduction of the teacher and the counselor, made for an informal atmosphere and a comfortable feeling for the audience. The supervisor then introduced the subject by first pointing out the importance of the work which was done to help the youngsters master the fundamentals. Quite a point was made of this because she did not wish the parents to think that the topic of the day was the only part of the school program.

Then she indicated that as these fundamentals were being taught, the teacher was employing methods which helped children to learn to work together and to develop good human relationships. She also indicated that while that school system had a highly developed guidance program, it was the teacher who had the youngster all day, every day, who knew him best and who did the greatest part of the guidance work with him.

The teacher took over at this point. She, too, began by reassuring the parents that the fundamentals were the core of the program, but she knew they would be interested in hearing about the other phases of the program as well.

Since the program was being held in her room, she kept bringing out things to illustrate what the children had been doing cooperatively. One amusing thing she showed them was a burro the children had made. She said that one member of the class was reluctant to get in on the act because she was afraid that she would be the one to have to sew up the burro's rear end and she might be embarrassed. When the teacher told her that it would take two or three people to do that, the child went right to work on the project. In showing these cooperatively made things, the teacher made a point of telling how the children planned them together, sharing ideas and laying out a master plan of operation, deciding who could do the best with each part. She also indicated that the children learned to appreciate what each one did and learned to express their appreciation. This, she said, made for good feeling among the group members and also helped the children to get into the habit of appreciating what others could do. By the time she had finished, all parents present were convinced that their children were not only being taught essential fundamentals but were also being well taught in the ways of democratic living.

The counselor spoke next. She explained to the parents that because teachers had such heavy loads, they were not always able to give the individual attention that some youngsters needed for their best development. For this reason counselors were employed in the school system. She pointed out that many youngsters found large groups too stimulating for them and consequently became hyperactive in the classroom. She had found that if she took them out of the room and worked quietly with them, they usually were able to go back into the room and settle down for the rest of the day. Others, who were fundamentally shy, seemed to blossom under the feeling of importance that they got from her individual attention. Still others, who had various problems which may have kept them from learning according to their ability, were frequently helped by the individual counseling that she was able to give them.

The counselor also explained the testing program— what the tests were all about, how the results were used to make the instructional program more effective, and how tests were used in the guidance of each individual child.

She indicated that she was more or less the coordinator of the records. The parents were quite impressed at the amount of information the counselor was able to gather about each child. They were particularly impressed when the teacher reassured them that only constructive information was retained in the folder. She took time out at this point to explain why the IQs were not given out to the parents, saying that results varied quite a bit according to the test, that an IQ was only a mathematical formula, that testing conditions sometimes influenced test results, and that sometimes, if parents knew the IQ, they either expected too much of their child—putting too much pressure on him—or, on the other hand, feeling that the child was not bright, became so discouraged that the child felt it. She said that in evaluating a child, the school used every bit of information available—test results, subject achievement, teachers' evaluation, objective observation, anecdotal notes, etc. It became clear to the parents, as she talked, that while use of the recorded IQ might be made in evaluating a child, it was not the only thing; its importance in their minds diminished to a great extent.

The counselor also indicated that one of her duties was to coordinate any special services that a child might need, providing whatever school information was required by a specific agency. She was the one who referred the youngster to the school psychologist. She was the one who made sure of parent approval and set up the conference between parents and the psychologist. Also, it was she who referred any child to the attendance counselor and often to the nurse or school doctor. She was the one who made sure that too many agencies didn't get in on the act at the same time.

By the time the counselor had finished talking, the parents were convinced not only that their children were being well taught, but that each child had a special friend besides his own teacher to watch over him as an individual.

The supervisor was the last one to speak. Since she was specifically connected with the special services of this school system, she picked up where the counselor had left off and gave the parents a picture of how the school psychologists and social workers operated, attempting in some degree to explain the use of testing, intensive counseling, and other procedures. She gave several specific examples showing how individual children had been helped to overcome their emotional problems. Next she indicated the difference between the work of the attendance counselors of today and that of the old "hooky cops" who used to drag the youngsters in by the hair of their heads. The goal of today's attendance officers is to discover the reason for truancy and to work with the students, the parents, and the school people to solve the problem presented. These attendance counselors are liaison people, well trained these days, whose primary interest is in helping young people to make a good adjustment. She quoted the number of homes contacted the previous year and cited the fine work the department had done in working cooperatively and constructively with the juvenile bureau and other agencies. All in all, here was a department taking a positive approach and one which contributed immeasurably to the welfare of children.

The health department, she felt, would be of interest to these parents. Did they know that their school system provided nurses, doctors, and dental hygienists for the benefit of their children? The doctors did not give treatment, but did examine children and make recommendations. The nurses followed up with the parents on these recommendations. The nurses' primary objective, however, was to promote good health habits among the youngsters. The same was true of the dentists and dental hygienists. The dentists examined the children's teeth and made recommendations to the parents; the hygienists cleaned teeth and helped the children to learn practices of good tooth care. The health department, then, made not only immediate contributions to the physical well-being of the children but also long-term contributions.

Finally, the supervisor spoke of the department of special education. Here was a department which provided for children who had severe physical or mental handicaps. Special classes, with highly trained teachers, were set up in rooms especially equipped to serve children who had orthopedic, hearing, and sight difficulties, so that they had maximum opportunities to develop up to their potential. Speech therapists went from school to school to help children overcome speech difficulties. Home teachers were provided for those who could not attend school at all.

Special classes, with specially trained teachers, were set up for mentally retarded children so that they, too, would have the opportunity to develop up to capacity. All educable children, then, in this school system were generously provided for.

In closing her presentation, the supervisor made a great point of letting the parents know that it was their support, their interest in the schools, which made it possible for all children to receive the splendid opportunities for education and academic, social, physical, and mental health development.

At this point she gave the parents an opportunity to ask questions of any member of the panel. Naturally, the parents had many questions. Some of them had heard vaguely about some of the special services. They were eager to know whether they themselves could initiate the request for help from these departments. Some were interested in hearing more about the regular daily classroom program. Still others wanted to know what they should do about their particular child's behavior. The panel members answered all but the last kind of question readily and well. The supervisor tactfully suggested that those parents who had specific questions about their own child might speak to the counselor during the social hour which would immediately follow.

This account of a team presentation illustrates most of the points mentioned at the beginning of the chapter. It was a good meeting in that the atmosphere was informal; the teacher had good materials at hand to illustrate the ways she helped children with their personal relationships; the counselor gave information which was quite new to most of the parents; and the supervisor told them many things that made them proud of their school system. There was good audience participation and an opportunity for individual chats with panel members after the meeting itself was over.

Let us think now of other meetings which teachers might have with parents. These will be discussed very briefly only to give the reader ideas for the kinds of programs which might be helpful for both parents and teacher and which will truly benefit the children.

A room mothers' meeting

One teacher tells of an interesting meeting she held with a group of mothers of eighth-grade children. The meeting had come about at the request of the mothers themselves. It seemed that the youngsters had been playing the various mothers against one another about how many times a week they should be allowed to go out and how late they should be allowed to stay. Each youngster would say, "But Sally's mother lets her stay out until one o'clock. You're going to make everybody think I'm a square if you don't let me stay out at least that late." The parents were quite distraught. They didn't feel that their children should go out so much or stay out so late, and yet they did not want to put their children at a social disadvantage with the others. Besides, the conflict over the issue made living with the children almost unbearable.

They sought the help of a young and popular junior high school teacher. After some discussion, they came to the conclusion that if the mothers would all get together on the matter, their children would not be so able to browbeat them. The teacher suggested that they have the meeting and invite several of the youngsters, not only to be present, but also to participate on a panel with the parents. Perhaps, together they could arrive at some reasonable agreement. Since it would be done cooperatively, the youngsters might be more willing to go along with the decision of the group. Also, since many parents and youngsters would be there when the decision was made, it would make it easier for all concerned. No one would be in a position to argue about what was considered fair.

The meeting was held in the evening so that fathers could attend also. The teacher, who had a delightful sense of humor, told two very clever jokes related to parent–teen-ager relationships. This helped to break the ice somewhat, although there still was evidence of considerable strain. She then went into a humorous bit of history on the perpetual problem of teen-age dating and parental concern, showing clearly that there was nothing new to be discussed this evening but merely a matter that was always of concern—both to the youngsters and to the parents. Tonight, however, this matter was going to be handled in a sensible way and, she hoped, some conclusions reached which would make life bearable once again in the many households represented there.

With this, she called on the youngsters, one by one (there were three on the panel), to present their point of view and to make suggestions as to how the matter could be handled best.

They did this quite ably. Some of their remarks were a little sharp but, on the whole, quite fair and certainly representative of the usual teen-age point of view.

Then the parents were asked to present their point of view. They, too, were fair in their remarks, and because they were not talking in their own homes to their own offspring with whom they were all tied up emotionally, they were able to point out quite objectively the concern that parents naturally had and why they felt the way they did about these matters.

There was back and forth discussion then among the panel members for a few minutes. Presently the teacher gave the audience a chance to comment. It was interesting that, having heard both sides of the problem, the audience participants, both parents and youngsters, made very constructive, unemotional contributions toward the solution of the problem. The whole group actually got together in their thinking and were able to set up reasonable and flexible regulations.

What a fine thing that teacher did! And how interesting it was to her to do it! It wasn't easy, and certainly not every teacher can do it. This one had the confidence of the youngsters as well as of the parents, and because of her good humor and way of working, she was able to get them together on something that was of utmost importance to both parties.

Specialists participate as consultants

Some teachers have felt the need of calling in specialists to act as consultants at some of their parent meetings. This was true in the case of a kindergarten teacher who had a spate of crying children in her room. She was beside herself wondering what to do to stem the tide. Finally, after trying all the tricks in her trade that she knew, she called on a school psychologist and a school social worker to meet with the parents of her children.

These were two able people who were very well versed in the field of child development. They were easy in their relationship to the group of mothers, not pretending to have all the answers, but rather expressing their desire to explore the problem with them.

The teacher outlined the situation in some detail, giving specific examples of the many crying episodes. Then she turned to the two specialists and asked them for comments. They immediately turned to the mothers and asked them whether this behavior was typical of the children at home, and then whether they had any ideas as to the causes of all this crying. Two or three mothers had some ideas to offer. After getting as many ideas as possible from the mothers themselves, the specialists made their contributions and recommendations.

The mothers and the teacher were very enthusiastic over the help they received. Although a great deal of child psychology came into the discussion, the specialists had brought it in so casually and easily that it sounded like just plain horse sense.

The mothers asked the teacher and the specialists whether they couldn't have a series of meetings with them on the subject of child development. Three subsequent meetings were arranged, and they proved to be so popular that other schools in the system began making requests for the specialists' time.

Teachers often get into situations which seem beyond them, and it is indeed fortunate when they can get the help of specialists. It is also fortunate when teachers recognize the fact that such specialists can be helpful and not a threat to them in any way.

Problems
of the mechanics

CHAPTER FOUR

Scheduling problems   Preliminary preparation and planning   For students   For parents   For teachers   Techniques of the interview   The teacher's reputation   Preparation for a specific interview   The art of listening   The frank approach   Sensitivity to the individual parent   Summary of insights or proposed action   The open door   Room for improvement   Evaluation leading to improvement   Evaluation sheets for parent-teacher conferences   Parent-teacher conferences in secondary school   Individual differences in students and parents   Conferences initiated by subject teachers   Conferences assigned to certain teachers   Short conferences with all the student's teachers   Conferences conducted by the homeroom sponsors   Conferences held at invitation of the teacher   How and when to schedule the interview   The home visit

Even while educators recognize the importance of parent-teacher conferences and feel that such conferences are essential to good education, many of them find it most difficult to work out an adequate schedule that allows time for them. After all, teachers have a full day. There is much content to be covered. What is to be done?

Scheduling problems

In the school districts where interest in parent-teacher conferences is high, time is provided for interviews of from fifteen to thirty minutes. It has been found that two or three different methods might be used to provide time. Some school systems run on a minimum day schedule over a period of time, letting the youngsters go home early and using the rest of the regular day schedule for the conferences. For example, one junior high school is dismissed at noon for one week, and fifteen- to twenty-minute interviews are scheduled. The teachers also spend one or two evenings a week in holding conferences for parents who cannot come to school during the day.

One superintendent persuaded the board of education to add eight days to the regular 180 days of school, with salary adjustments for the extra days. Three of these days were devoted to parent conferences and five to workshops for teachers.

In other districts, the principal, vice-principal, and counselor take the teacher's classes for a period or two a day over a certain length of time, thus releasing the teacher for her interviews. Teachers are also freed for parent-teacher conferences by having an assembly or athletic program for the whole school; this can be supervised by several teachers.

In a few school systems, mostly experimental programs, "master teachers" or special teachers conduct classes for large groups, freeing the regular teacher for individual conferences with students and parents, for in-service education, and for other special activities. In less-progressive districts, parent-teacher conferences are held on teacher time. The teachers feel that these conferences mean so much to them that they are willing to stay for a half hour after school over some period of time to talk to parents.

These blocks of time are usually in the fall and again in the early spring, depending upon the number of parent conferences systematically held during the year. In most school systems that provide for a program of parent-teacher conferences, it is considered quite important to have one conference at the end of the first period of "reporting" time. It is felt that it helps the teacher to understand the student's total behavior early enough to do some good; that it helps the teacher to gain close working relationships with the parent, which prove invaluable in working out problems later during the school year; and that it helps the child from the beginning to think of the school and the home as cooperative, not antagonistic, as some children think.

Preliminary preparation and planning

For students

It is extremely important that the child or adolescent understand the reason for the conference, that he know that this is not to be an occasion for two or more adults to gang up on him. It has been found valuable to invite the student to sit in on the conference and make his contribution. It is surprising how much insight some children and adolescents have into their learning problems and their behavior problems also. Far from being embarrassed, they often seem to be stimulated by the attention given to their opinions and welcome the opportunity to speak frankly. Such three-way conferences have proved to be the turning point in a student's life at school. They may, however, be difficult to manage and require more skill than the usual parent-teacher conference.

If students understand and are interested in the parent-teacher conference, the invitations to parents may be sent home through their children. In other situations letters are mailed to the parents.

For parents

When the actual program for the conferences is set up, parents need to be brought in on the planning. They need to understand what it is all about and to feel that this is a cooperative venture which is going to be beneficial to their child and to their understanding of the school program. In one school system all parents received a detailed questionnaire asking their opinion concerning the purpose of the parent-teacher conference, its content, how they would like to have it scheduled and conducted, and the value it would be to them. The parents' interest was indicated by a high percentage of replies and by thoughtful responses. A comparable questionnaire was filled out by teachers. All replies were carefully tabulated by a committee of parents, and a summary was presented for discussion at a parent-teacher meeting. This procedure provided the basis for the successful program of parent-teacher conferences that was introduced after this year of preliminary planning.

Whatever the method used to gain acceptance and understanding of the idea, usually a letter such as the following is sent home:

Dear Mr. and Mrs. —————:

Both parents and teachers at Fremont School have expressed a wish for a closer relationship between school and home. We all agree, I am sure, that a conference between a child's teacher and his parents is one means of strengthening that relationship.

Because you have expressed an interest in this, we are planning to schedule parent conferences in place of the comments on the next report card. Miss ————— is one of several teachers at Fremont who have indicated their desire to participate in this plan; we hope that you will share her interest in your child.

At a later date we will suggest a tentative schedule of appointments, giving you a choice of the most convenient day and hour. Please feel welcome to comment on this arrangement. Your ideas and suggestions can help us all.

Sincerely,

Mary Conway, *Principal*

A short time later such a letter is followed by another, which gives the parent a chance to make a convenient appointment. Such a letter might be set up as follows:

Dear Mr. and Mrs. ——————:

We should like to schedule your conference with your child's teacher at the time most convenient for you. Will you please indicate your first, second, and third choices of the days listed below and return your answer as soon as possible. Thank you.

——————————————
                                            Principal

Choice:

( )   March 3, 1:30
( )   March 5, 2:00
( )   March 9, 3:00

——————————————
                              Signature of Parent

After the parent has indicated the most convenient time for him to appear at the school, the following brief note can be sent:

Dear Mr. and Mrs. ——————:

Your appointment with your child's teacher was scheduled for

——————.

We hope that you will find this time convenient. If, for any reason, it is not, will you kindly let us know so that we may set up another appointment for you. Thank you.

——————————————
                                            Principal

For teachers

Parent-teacher conferences should not be initiated without preliminary preparation for the teachers. Like parents, they need to gain more understanding of the purpose and procedures of the parent-teacher conference and the interpretation of test results. They should also have a part in planning the program. If they feel that they are an important part of the educational program, they will participate in it with more interest and enthusiasm.

Sometimes a committee of teachers are interested in studying the problem and report to the faculty as a whole.

The wise administrator often talks with teachers individually to correct misunderstanding, to dispel misgivings, and to minimize initial antagonisms before he introduces the subject in a general faculty meeting. He knows that if a teacher gets up and expresses a negative point of view in a meeting, that teacher will not later want to admit that he was wrong. Accordingly the administrator will proceed wisely and slowly in developing the program cooperatively.

Still more effective is some form of study group in which a more thorough understanding of the parent-teacher conference can be obtained. In one school system, a workshop on parent-teacher conferences was attended on a voluntary basis by about fifty teachers. It was held after school one day a week for ten weeks. The sessions included the following:

Problems of communication between parents and teachers.

Examples of parent attitudes and how to respond to them.

Content of different kinds of parent-teacher conferences, factual information, and sources of information often requested by parents.

A panel discussion by parents of gifted, average, and under-achieving students invited by the teachers to consider the parents' role and the kind of conference they appreciate most. (This session was a most interesting and enlightening one to both teachers and parents.)

Dramatized reading of various kinds of parent-teacher interviews, each followed by a discussion of the interview technique and how the parent may have felt during and at the end of the interview.

Role playing of various interview situations, as the members of the group became willing to obtain this kind of preliminary practice.

Careful preplanning and training helps to ensure successful conferences. It develops security, readiness, and enthusiasm on the part of all concerned.

Techniques of the Interview

Throughout the book excerpts of actual interviews, followed by comments as to why they were or were not effective, supplement the generalizations to be presented here about the preparation for and conduct of parent-teacher conferences.

The teacher's reputation

The initial rapport and success of the interview depend more than we like to think on the parent's preconceived idea of the teacher derived from what her Johnny has said and from what other mothers think of him. Such mind-sets influence the parents' expectations of the help they will get from the interview, their willingness to speak frankly, and their acceptance of any suggestions that may be given. It is difficult, but not impossible, for the teacher to change an initially unfavorable attitude by his sincerity, good sense, and considerateness for the parent during the interview.

Preparation for a specific interview

In Chapter 5 we shall see that a teacher might be at a disadvantage in an unscheduled interview. If he knows a parent is coming at a particular time, the teacher can bring together and synthesize his understanding of the parent's child, note topics that would be likely to evoke a favorable response, and avoid topics that might interfere with establishing an initially friendly relationship.

The teacher can also formulate hypotheses as to the most important aspects of the child's development to discuss in the limited interview time. He can have dated samples of the child's work to illustrate progress along certain lines. To be sure to discuss the points of most importance, the teacher might formulate certain questions he would like to ask. Preparation of this kind serves as a guide, not as a blueprint, for the interview.

The art of listening

Most teachers talk too much. In a short interview with parents, this tendency often becomes pronounced just because they are so eager to give the parent as much help as possible in the short time available. If they realize that listening may be the greatest help to both parent and teacher and that the success of an interview depends upon how much the parent gains in insight and intent, rather than on how much he is told, they will feel less impelled to give unsolicited advice.

A teacher who listens intently, who convinces the parents that he is comprehending how they are thinking and feeling, and who shows by his words and expression that he considers this conference the most important thing he could be doing, stimulates parents to do their best thinking and to seek solutions for the problems they have presented.

The frank approach

Although the teacher should not begin an interview with criticism of the child, many parents say, at least, that they want to know the truth about their child; they prefer a frank approach. If he is having trouble in school, they want to know it.

Much depends on the kind of criticism and the way in which it is given. Only harm is accomplished by negative criticism about which the parents can do nothing. Constructive criticism in which the difficulty or deficiency is introduced by some concrete suggestion for dealing with it is often welcomed.

Sensitivity to the individual parent

No rule of thumb or prescription for conducting a parent-teacher conference can be given. There is no substitute for continuous sensitivity to the way the individual parent is thinking and feeling. By observing his facial expression and bodily movements as well as by listening to what he says and noting what he fails to communicate, the teacher can get clues as to the effectiveness of his approach.

Summary of insights or proposed action

Often parents leave the conference with dissatisfaction. They feel that nothing has been done to make them aware of what has actually been accomplished. It is a good idea for the teacher to summarize the main points. He may reinforce an insight the parent has briefly mentioned; repeat, sometimes in a slightly more feasible form, a plan the parent thought might work; or review the slightly different, more hopeful view of his child that he has acquired.

Another purpose of a brief summary is accurate communication of the content of the conference to the parent who was not able to attend. Usually it is the mother who can come to the school; she will tell her husband what the teacher said about their child. A summary is a great help to her in reporting the important outcome of the conference.

The open door

At the end of the interview, it is usually well to suggest a return visit if the parents desire one. If a plan has been proposed, the possibility of coming back to report how it worked is an additional incentive to the parents to carry out the plan. Also it is reassuring just to know there is someone to whom they can turn if their child does not make the expected progress.

Room for improvement

Teachers feel a real need for help in actually conducting the parent conferences. How do they open the interview? What kind of approach do they make? What kinds of thing do they say? How do they close, etc., etc.? The following chapters are intended to give specific help in regard to the many different kinds of interviews which teachers are called upon to conduct. Perhaps the reader can benefit from reading accounts of actual interviews of the type most difficult for him.

Evaluation leading to improvement

The following two evaluation reports contain a wealth of specific suggestions for planning and conducting parent-teacher conferences, based on the first year's experience with parent-teacher conferences.

After the first year in which her school had participated in such a program, Marion Wells, then principal of the Fremont Elementary School in Long Beach, California, made the following report to the assistant superintendent in charge of the elementary schools:

Here is a brief summary of the parent conference experiment which we carried on during the month of March. Three teachers were chosen to participate. We first met to decide the approximate length of each conference and to share some of the ideas we had for conducting them.

The teachers decided that half an hour was a good length of time for a conference, although some parents would require more and some less. They all remarked that the key word was "listen," and they all went into the program with the idea of learning from the parent rather than the other way around. Each teacher planned to work at least one evening, thus making it possible for working mothers to attend. The teachers checked each report card and in place of "Teacher's Remarks" wrote "Conference."

Miss Bacon, the sixth-grade teacher, held her conferences from March 1 to 10, working seven afternoons from one to four, and one evening from seven to nine. I taught her class each day. She talked with thirty-one mothers, seven fathers, and one grandmother. Only two parents did not keep their appointments. There were many expressions of satisfaction from parents about experiences their children had had in Miss Bacon's room, and also with the parent conference in lieu of a report card.

Miss Wright and Mrs. Kulp, the junior first- and first-grade teachers, decided to hold conferences on alternate days. We had a substitute for two weeks, releasing them from their rooms for one-half day. Miss Wright talked with twenty-six parents and Mrs. Kulp talked with thirty-three parents. Both had an attendance of 100 per cent. Each teacher reported parent satisfaction with the schoolroom experiences as well as with the parent conferences.

The teachers, in evaluating their conferences, felt that they had gained much valuable information about their children and that even though they were emotionally more exhausted than when they wrote report cards, the value received was well worth the extra effort.

They would all like to continue the program next year, with an early fall conference, possibly followed by one in the spring. They found that they needed ten or fifteen minutes between conferences to record their impressions and to collect their thoughts for the next parent.

Several parents who have other children in rooms not participating in the conferences have asked whether a conference might be substituted for a report card.

I should like very much to repeat the program next year, with the addition of two more very mature teachers at the fourth- and sixth-grade levels. Several teachers have indicated a willingness to hold conferences, but I should like to follow an in-service training program such as San Bernardino (California) and other schools use before making it a school-wide project.

Teachers in the Eugene Field Elementary School, in the same district, made the following random comments during their evaluation period after they had participated for the first time in a similar program:

1. We need help to prepare for the conferences. There is a need to learn how we can talk to parents of their child's ability or inability—telling of our testing program, assuring them that we do have records, etc.
2. We should like to have the school nurse sit in on our conferences if there is a health problem involved.
3. We should like to have the principal or counselor sit in on a conference when the parent is known to be difficult or when the child has a severe behavior problem. We think that the teacher needs to avoid getting too deep in the why and wherefore if the problem is psychological.
4. We need to help the parent to leave the conference with the feeling that there are immediate plans to help the child.
5. We think it is important to be a good listener if the mother has a problem and wants to tell it in her way.
6. A brief form should be worked out for the teacher to record objectively the report of the conference. This could be kept in the child's cumulative record.
7. The children should have an understanding of, and know the reason for, the conference—that it is not to report "bad behavior."
8. We need to be relieved more in some way to allow for time to hold the conference.
9. We should plan for interpretation if the home has foreign-language-speaking parents.
10. The children's work should be kept during the year to use in helping to explain both the school program and the child's progress in school.
11. Provision should be made for a follow-up conference when parents or teachers feel such need.
12. Provision should be made for evening conferences for working parents.

13. We should use the report card as a springboard with the parent. A card or a duplicate could be taken home for the father's perusal if he has been unable to attend the conference.

14. If we're going to have a substitute to give us released time, we should have her every afternoon or every morning, rather than alternating, so as to ensure better teaching continuity.

15. We should prefer to have the conferences after school to avoid making lesson plans for a substitute.

16. To prevent interruption, we need to work out some plan to take care of the little children that the parents bring along.

17. It is surprising how the parents can face reality.

18. We have a much better understanding of our children now.

19. We found that many parents came for this conference who never came for anything else. Maybe those who didn't come could be visited in their homes.

20. We should have in mind everything that we know about a given child before we enter into this conference.

The above-mentioned comments were made in an informal group meeting. No special pattern for evaluation or for ideas to be used in the future was used. However, all these comments were considered individually and in groups and proved to be helpful for the following year.

Some school systems ask their teachers to use a regular evaluation sheet for the parent-teacher conferences, such as the following:

Evaluation sheets for parent-teacher conferences

1. Were the parents cooperative?
   _____ Yes _____ No
2. Did the parents express their ideas easily?
   _____ Yes _____ No

3. Did you gain insights into their children's behavior?
_____ Yes _____ No

4. Do you feel the parents obtained adequate understanding of where their child stood in the subject-matter field?
_____ Yes _____ No

5. Was it possible to formulate cooperatively constructive plans for future adjustment?
_____ Yes _____ No

6. Was it satisfying to be able to give the parents a true picture of the child's work and ability?
_____ Yes _____ No

7. Did you find parents to whom you could not give a complete picture of the child's behavior at school?
_____ Yes _____ No

8. List: A. Number of conferences scheduled _____
        B. Number of conferences parents canceled _____
        C. Number of parents who failed to appear at the scheduled time _____

9. Would you welcome further conferences?
_____ Yes _____ No

10. Did you gain personal family information that was best not to include on written reports?
_____ Yes _____ No

11. Did you find it easy to determine the pertinent facts to be included on written reports?
_____ Yes _____ No

12. Would you like in-service training for the conferences?
_____ Yes _____ No

13. Do you feel you need in-service training for the conferences?
_____ Yes _____ No

Such sheets can be very helpful in guiding the thinking of the teachers as they review their experiences, but, perhaps, after the sheets have been used, an informal group discussion among all the teachers who participated in the program would be helpful.

It is also important to get the reaction of the parents to the conferences. It often serves as the basis of fine discussions, either in a grade-level meeting or in a regular PTA meeting. However, in order to get reactions from more parents, some school systems send them a regular evaluation sheet like the following:

Parent-Teacher Conferences ＿＿＿＿＿＿ Elementary School

Dear Parents:

Recently you were asked to participate in parent-teacher conferences to discuss the progress of your child in school. In order that we may know what can be done to improve these meetings, we should like you to check the questions below. You need not sign your name. Will you please return your questionnaire in the enclosed envelope:

1. Did you enjoy going to school to talk with your child's teacher?
＿＿＿＿ Yes ＿＿＿＿ No
2. Did you like the conference better than the report card?
＿＿＿＿ Yes ＿＿＿＿ No
3. Did you understand better your child's progress in:

Reading __ Yes __ No	Arithmetic __ Yes __ No
Writing __ Yes __ No	Spelling __ Yes __ No
Music __ Yes __ No	Games __ Yes __ No
Art __ Yes __ No	Social studies __ Yes __ No

4. Did you and the teacher make plans to work together with your child?
＿＿＿＿ Yes ＿＿＿＿ No
5. Do you understand the school program better?
＿＿＿＿ Yes ＿＿＿＿ No
6. Do you understand better how your child gets along with his classmates?
＿＿＿＿ Yes ＿＿＿＿ No
7. Do you feel that because of this exchange of information both you and the teacher know more about your child?
＿＿＿＿ Yes ＿＿＿＿ No
8. Would you welcome another conference with your child's teacher?
＿＿＿＿ Yes ＿＿＿＿ No

Using the results of informal evaluation discussions, together with evaluation sheets from both the teachers and the parents, a planning group composed of both these groups might well sit down and think through plans for the next year. The more the parents participate in the planning, the more successful the conferences are likely to be. Too, as parents express their interest, teachers get the feeling that the conferences are most worthwhile, and consequently they are more willing to give their time and effort.

Parent-teacher conferences in secondary school

Teachers and students at the secondary level can also benefit from parent conferences. The purpose and problems are similar to those in elementary school, but they are somewhat wider in range and often more difficult to solve.

Individual differences in students and parents

In secondary school, teachers encounter students who are not achieving up to capacity—those who seem to be laboring under too much pressure, those who present long-standing behavior problems, those who are waiting for the day when they will be old enough to get out of school, those who do not seem to have appropriate vocational goals, those who are very withdrawn, those who are very superior and need more challenge at home and at school.

Individual differences in parents must also be given consideration. Is this a parent who will make life miserable for the child after a conference? Is this a parent who will be cooperative? Is this parent one who might put too much pressure on the child? Is the relationship between the parent and child such that the conference will prove helpful or damaging? Is this a working parent who will resent the school's insisting that he take time off from work for such a conference?

Conferences initiated by subject teachers

When secondary teachers teach some two hundred youngsters per day instead of thirty or forty as in the elementary school, it is obviously impossible for them to have parent conferences with all the students they teach. Yet many do contact the parents of some of their students.

It is impossible to specify exactly what kind of youngster would benefit most from a conference between his teacher and his parent. It would depend so much on what was known about the parent and his relationships with his child. Also, teachers differ greatly in their own feelings about the problems that youngsters present. Some teachers are most concerned about behavior problems. Others manage behavior problems very well but are baffled by children who have good ability but are underachieving. Still others are concerned with the shy, withdrawn youngster who seems always to be outside the group. Therefore it is natural that the type of conference would probably depend on teachers' individual preferences.

Conferences assigned to certain teachers

A good way to make selections of parents to be contacted by certain teachers is that practiced in many schools: All the teachers of a given grade level, freshman, sophomore, junior, or senior, are asked by the counselor or administrator to submit the names of three students who they feel present some kind of problem.[1] If a student's name is turned in two or more times, the counselor invites all the teachers of that youngster to meet for a few minutes, either before or after school, or at a special table in the cafeteria during the lunch hour. There the teachers share information about the student—how well he does in each of their classes, what kind of behavior he presents, what is known about

[1] "Problem" here is defined as any condition interfering with the student's best development.

his parents and brothers and sisters, whether he is underachieving, etc. The counselor supplements the information that the teachers have and, in addition, summarizes the comments made by the teachers.

Almost always, in this type of conference, it is found that the youngster is closer to one teacher than to the others. If the pooled information reveals that a parent-teacher conference would be helpful, it is usually best for that particular teacher to invite the parent to come to school. However, it is also quite all right for one other teacher or the counselor to sit in on the conference. More than two school people probably should not meet with the parent at one time. Parents tend to be anxious when they are talking to teachers, and to be confronted by a whole array of them makes them most uncomfortable.

Again, what should be made clear to the student involved is that the conference will take place and that the reason for it is not to report bad behavior but to attempt to work out something which would be beneficial to his growth and development. In some schools the student council has been helpful in convincing the student body of the positive nature of the parent-teacher conference. Sometimes the student is invited to sit in on the conference and contribute to it, if this seems wise. This decision, again, emphasizes the importance of the teacher's knowing something of the student's previous development and home background before launching into a conference. Usually this information can be obtained in the above-mentioned conference of all the student's teachers or from the counselor's records.

Helpful information may also be contained in the cumulative folder. It is also possible that the counselor and/or vice-principal has worked with this individual previously. If so, they undoubtedly have quite a bit of information about the home situation. They are in a good position to be very helpful to the teacher. Counselors, vice-principals, and teachers must always remember that the conference is to benefit the child through the sharing of helpful information and constructive planning, not to place blame or full responsibility on the parent. The welfare is paramount. If the conference is considered potentially good for him, on the basis of all information, it will be wise to hold it; if it is likely to be damaging to him, either through causing a strain in his relationship with his parents or by making him resent school, then the conference should not be held. The conferences must have positive results. Naturally, in the case of extreme behavior problems, it does become necessary to ask the parents to share in the responsibility which such problems place on the school, but, in general, the individual youngster must receive first consideration.

Short conferences with all the student's teachers

In one junior high school, parent conferences are scheduled in a large room where all the subject teachers are comfortably seated and easily identified. Parents have a period of five minutes to talk to each of their child's teachers. Almost three-fourths of the parents attended these conferences and expressed satisfaction in having this opportunity to talk even briefly with each teacher.

Conferences conducted by the homeroom sponsors

In this form of organization, on the high school level, conferences were held with the parents of every student. In preparation for the conference, every subject teacher made a half-page summary on the strengths, needs, and suggestions for improvement for each student. The summaries were given to the homeroom sponsor, who coordinated the information. After conducting the interview, the homeroom sponsor summarized the main points and filed the summary in the student's cumulative record folder.

Conferences held at invitation of the teacher

When a teacher notices the first signs of a student's failure in academic work or social adjustment, which may be prevented by home-school cooperation, he may initiate a conference with the parents. Many teachers have always done this. The focus of such interviews is developmental rather than remedial. It is concerned with the individual's self-realization. Parents and adolescents both appreciate this positive emphasis—so different from the negative approach typical of parent conferences in the past.

How and when to schedule the interview

In most secondary school systems, teachers have what is known as a "free" period or a "conference" period. Wise administrators make it clear that these periods are set up for the benefit of the students, that every student should have access to his teacher for individual help if need be. Since the parent conferences are considered to be beneficial to the students involved, this is a legitimate time for the conferences to be held. Sometimes, however, when parents cannot get to school during that time, other time must be provided.

Some secondary school administrators feel that these conferences are so important that they, like the elementary administrators, provide for released teacher time, either by providing substitutes or by running minimum days, sending the students home early and leaving the teacher free to meet the parents.

Teachers have for years, of course, met with parents on their own time just because of sheer interest in the youngster involved. Parents are almost invariably appreciative of the time these teachers take, and they are cooperative in their attitude.

The home visit

Some teachers even arrange to go to the home of the parents. This is quite all right as long as the teacher is tactful and the parents are prepared for the visit. Dropping in on parents without warning is taboo. It might be a most inconvenient time for a busy mother or father; or the house might not be so clean and orderly as the mother would like it to be when her child's teacher comes to call; this would cause real embarrassment and even resentment. It is only courteous, then, to telephone or write a note asking permission to call.

Of all the single sources of information obtained by counselors in University High School, Oakland, California, in connection with their adolescent study, they thought home visits gave them the most valuable understanding of the adolescent.

After any conference, whether held at school or in the home, the teacher should write a brief summary of what went on, giving a carbon copy to the counselor, at whose discretion it may or may not be included in the student's cumulative folder.

Parents come to school
on their own

CHAPTER FIVE

Values of the voluntary conference Alerting teacher to the child's needs Modifying initial antagonism Attempting to ascertain the problem Clarifying a problem and finding a solution

Often teachers have fears of parents dropping in on them out of the blue. When parents come for a conference with teachers at inopportune times, it is more than disconcerting. The worst time is during class period. The teacher's instruction of the class is interrupted; the pupils are distracted; some may become unruly; and the child or adolescent whose mother suddenly appears in class is usually intensely embarrassed. Under such conditions the conference is, of necessity, hurried and superficial.

Even when the parent comes unexpectedly during a teacher's free period or after school, the teacher is at a disadvantage. He has not had time to think about and interpret that particular child's progress and problems. He has not been able to obtain clues from the cumulative record as to topics he might introduce or avoid. There has not been time to collect dated samples of the student's work or reports from other teachers that might give the parent concrete evidence of his child's achievement.

There are some advantages, however, in having parents drop in unexpectedly. They usually have a definite reason for their visit. Consequently they may have a greater readiness and receptivity for any help the teacher can give them. It is the parents who take the initiative rather than the teacher. This fact tends to dispel any authoritarian atmosphere that might prevail when the parents are asked to come to the school. The unscheduled conference might also have the advantage of nondirective counseling insofar as the teacher has no choice but to let the parents present themselves and their problems in their own way.

Values of the voluntary conference

In most cases, even when parents come in unexpectedly, the good teacher, through graciousness and understanding, can usually help parents to get a better picture of their child and, as a result of the conference, do a better job with the child. Excerpts from several interviews will illustrate some of the values that may be derived from the parent-initiated interview.

Alerting teacher to the child's needs

One teacher writes about how the unexpected visit of a Japanese mother helped her to concentrate more on the child's needs. It is interesting to see what took place and how she worked it all out.

The girl whom I shall call Michi Takahashi was ten years old. At the end of the first month of school, Michi's mother came to my classroom one afternoon just as the children were leaving. I invited her to come in, offered her a chair, and expressed my pleasure at her coming. Mrs. T. was most difficult to understand because of her broken English. I began the conversation by speaking of the fine work Michi was doing. Then I went to Michi's desk and showed her mother some of the work which Michi had been keeping in her folder. She nodded in approval. The gist of the conversation followed this pattern:

Mrs. T.: *Michi happy here.*

Teacher: *I'm so glad she likes us, because we think Michi is such a lovely girl. She does good work, too.*

Mrs. T.: *She like you.*

Teacher: *Maybe she knows I like her. I really do like to work with someone like Michi.*

Mrs. T.: *But she so shy. Her sister quiet, but not so much like Michi.*

Teacher: *Mrs. T., if I remember correctly, Michi is not with the same children that she was with last year. That may be one reason why Michi does not make friends in this group. When she knows and understands the children better, she will like to be with them more.*

Mrs. T.: *Yes* (nodding many times).

Teacher: *I don't want to overurge her right at this time, Mrs. T.; it is still early in the school year. I don't want her to be more self-conscious. I'm sure we shall be able to help her overcome her shyness if we move slowly. I'd rather not talk to Michi about it, but see that she has lots of chances to take part.*

Mrs. T.: *Thank you, thank you.*

The mother made several polite bows and kept thanking me profusely on her way out of the room. I invited her to come again soon. I also told her that I would contact her from time to time to let her know just what progress we were making. (Michi had been waiting on the steps during the interview. She had gone out voluntarily.)

My conclusion, following the short talk with Michi's mother, was that the child's timidity was a social adjustment in which I was sure the school could be helpful. Here was a challenge to us in the classroom.

The parent's short, unscheduled visit made the teacher more aware than she had been of the mother's concern for her child and the child's increasing shyness. After the interview, instead of before as in anticipated interviews, the teacher consulted the cumulative record and began to collect pertinent information.

Michi's IQ on a group intelligence test was 123; her reading grade, 8.4; and her arithmetic grade, 7.2. Michi was the younger of two daughters in this Japanese family. The father was a gardener; the mother did seasonal work at a cannery. Because of the mother's limited knowledge of the English language, she was attending night classes to learn our language better. The mother was very cooperative, interested, and most appreciative. The father had never visited school.

The mother's visit made me more observant of the child in the class. I noted that Michi is a beautiful child, very well cared for and dressed in good taste. She is small, but healthy, and has good coordination. Her attendance has been almost perfect—with only one day's absence. She is a perfectionist in all her work and is a beautiful writer. Michi is very artistic. She seems to have a natural talent for color harmony, perspective, balance, and proportion. She uses great care and planning in her work. She is an independent worker, follows directions well, and seldom asks me for help. She is well liked by her classmates, and her work gains recognition and praise from the group.

When Michi enters the room she comes in very quickly and quietly, walking in a semicircle rather than passing directly in front of anyone. She side-steps down the aisle in order to avoid touching a desk, person, or anything on the way to her seat. Her voice is very soft. In a group discussion —reading, social studies, science, etc.—she rarely contributes orally. If she is called upon, she answers as briefly as possible in a word or two.

My increased understanding of Michi from her mother's brief interview, the cumulative record, and my own observations led to providing experiences to help her overcome her shyness. At first she did not respond to my attempts to bring her more actively into the group. When she was offered a monitorship, she refused. As other children took turns playing the autoharp, Michi did not wish to participate. She chose to read a library book instead of playing a rhythm instrument as others were doing. On every possible occasion I carried on a brief one-sided conversation with her so that she would know of my friendly feeling toward her. I asked her about her sister in junior high school, Saturday matinees, etc.

Several days after the interview with her mother, Miss B., the librarian, asked for two girls to help her in the library during the lunch hour. I asked Barbara, a very dependable girl, and Michi whether they would be willing to help Miss B. Barbara accepted with enthusiasm, but Michi was hesitant. Barbara said, "Let's do it, Michi! We'll get to see all the new books as they come in." Michi said nothing, but her eyes told me she had accepted. The ice was broken! For twenty minutes every day they helped in the library. (I discussed Michi with the librarian.)

During a lesson in social studies, I very carefully placed Michi on a committee of girls only. (She was not yet ready to accept boys.) She wrote her information and gave it to the committee chairman.

Later I planned an exchange during a physical education period with another teacher—he took the boys, and I the girls. I took the girls to the auditorium for folk dancing. The girls were to choose another girl for a partner. I asked Barbara to choose Michi. Again Michi accepted. Having worked with Barbara in the library, she would, I felt, probably be more willing to accept Barbara. We made no fuss or even mention of the fact that Michi was dancing.

Still later the class was planning a mural which would show various phases of colonial life in New England. During the preceding art lesson, each child at his desk was painting something which he felt would be appropriate for use on the mural. During the evaluation, Michi's picture was the unanimous choice of the group to go on the mural first. Lonnie's was next choice. Many other pictures were chosen to be used. "Who should be chairman of the mural committee?" Perhaps we could have cochairmen—a boy and a girl. Michi and Lonnie were chosen. Another boy and girl completed the committee. Again Michi accepted! This was the first time she had worked with boys! Another step on the way.

Gradually and slowly, step by step, Michi was beginning to participate in a more active way, and she was enjoying it! She was losing her self-consciousness; she was becoming more social with others in the group.

She is now playing the autoharp to accompany class singing and doing an excellent job, she takes an active part in games, she is dancing with a boy as her partner, she talks much more frequently and in a stronger voice, and she has volunteered for monitor duty in the girls' lavatory. I am sure she is much happier because she belongs and is accepted as an active participant by the group.

This development in Michi's personality was not accomplished in ten easy lessons. It covered a period of seven or eight months. She is still quiet, but she is actively participating. I was indeed happy when I wrote on Michi's report card, "We appreciate the very fine work Michi is doing in all areas, but we are most happy because Michi is overcoming her shyness and is taking a much more active part in all our class activities."

It is obvious in this case that we have a skillful, sensitive teacher. Think of the good that came of the brief but friendly interview between the mother and the teacher. The interview is too brief to analyze other than to indicate the obvious—that the teacher's graciousness and manifested interest and liking for the child made the mother very happy. The mother's concern for the girl's shyness, which prompted her to come to school on her own initiative, helped the teacher to become more aware of this and to take more definite steps to help Michi relate herself to other children.

A voluntary visit by a parent who is friendly toward the

school is, of course, relatively easy for a teacher to work through. Excerpts from the next interview show quite a contrast—really quite a difficult situation.

Modifying initial antagonism

Giving a parent opportunity to blow off steam as it generates sometimes avoids an explosion. Obtaining some clarification of a grievance in its early stages may save a child from decisions detrimental to him. These needs cannot wait for scheduled conferences.

The following interview with an angry father concerned 8½-year-old Susan, who was in the low third grade. She was shy, withdrawn, and reading in a first-grade reader. Tests showed she was slow in learning school subjects. Because of lack of achievement, poor social adjustment, and immaturity, it seemed wise to retain her for another year in the third grade. A note to this effect was sent home, whereupon the father came storming to school. He was referred to Susan's teacher, Miss Dazey, by the clerk in the school office.

Miss Dazey: *I'm so glad that you came to talk about Susan and her work.*

Father: *You're glad? Well, I don't mind telling you that I'm plenty burned up about this note that you sent home about Susie. What do you mean she might not pass? Of course she'll pass. I'm not going to have any kid of mine sittin' in the same room two terms. It's your job to teach this child. I know she's a good girl. She'd better be! She's good at home. And I know she can read 'cause she reads all the time. Do you think there's something the matter with her that you're not going to pass her?*

Miss Dazey: *Susan is a very good little girl. She's such good help with keeping our room neat and feeding our pets.*

Father: *Doesn't seem as if she can learn anything doing that. She gets plenty of practice workin' at home. My wife's tired after taking care of the baby all day, and so Susie takes Patty after school so her Mom can get a breathin' spell. 'Course, she helps some with dinner, too. We eat early before I leave for the aircraft plant at six. And she washes the dishes. She's lots of help to her Mom, but that's what a kid's supposed to do. And she knows she'd catch it if she didn't. Now, what's wrong with her reading at school? Why don't you make her learn like you're supposed to? By golly, I can make her do things. And you're paid to do that!*

Miss Dazey: *I'm sure you want Susan to do her schoolwork well and to be a happy little girl, don't you?*

Father: *What d'you mean happy? She's happy, isn't she? I haven't heard her complain about not being happy.*

Miss Dazey: *Does Susan play much with other children around in the neighborhood, Mr. Hight?*

Father: *Oh, I guess so. There aren't many kids near us who are her age. And she's got too much to do at home to run down the street to play. What difference does that make to her read-ing? And anyway I think she can read good enough. . . . You think she doesn't read well enough, don't you?*

Miss Dazey: *She doesn't read as well as I think she can. She is not reading in a second-grade book yet, and I think she would be most unhappy in a higher grade, where the work is even harder, until she can read better. And perhaps she could get along better with children just a little younger than herself and play with them better. I'm sure you don't want to push her ahead until she is ready.*

Father: *Well, how can we make her ready? She can't be sticking around in the third grade forever!*

Miss Dazey: *You know, we have a playground director here at school every afternoon through the week from three to five o'clock. Many of the children from Susan's room stay here to play. Mrs. Harris, the director, is very helpful with them. She teaches them many games which they play in groups. I feel Susan would enjoy that and it would help her a great deal. Too, if she could play with neighbor children, even if they were younger, it would help her to overcome some of her shyness, perhaps, and also to develop some skills.*

Father: *Do you really think learning to play will make Susie read better? If you do, I suppose maybe her Mom could get along without her two or three evenings a week. I'll see what she says.*

Miss Dazey: *I think it will help her be a happier little girl to feel she belongs to our group activities. That seems very important to a child. She should also, then, find reading more fun to do with other children. Yes, I really think it will help her reading.*

Father: *Well, you may be right. You seem to have a new angle there, and I guess Susie doesn't read any too well. Maybe I was a little hasty getting so fired up about that note. Maybe Susie should have more time to play. And maybe it would be better if she stayed back and learned to read better before she gets lost. My wife wasn't too much of a student herself. Guess Susie kind of takes after her. She ought to understand about holding Susie back. Anyhow, I can persuade her, if you're sure that's the right thing to do. You are, huh?*

Miss Dazey: *Yes, I do think it's the best thing to do. It surely is a pleasure to talk to an understanding father who wants his little girl to be happy and to be in the best possible place for her in school. Thank you so much for coming. I hope Susan's mother will be able to come and see us soon. Susan would love that. The children always like to have their parents come to visit.*

Father: *I'll tell her to. Well, good-bye. I have to hurry to to get dinner and get off to work on time.*

Miss Dazey: *Good-bye, Mr. Hight!*

Let's review the things that happened in this interview:

FIRST   The teacher didn't let the anger of the father, confronting her so suddenly, throw her. She was still very courteous and seemingly just accepted the fact that the father was angry and calmly went on with the conversation.

SECOND She did not get on the defensive, but rather she directed the father's attention to an objective observation about his child's behavior, which conveyed her understanding of and concern for his child. This didn't appear to help matters much at the moment but perhaps it was just a little disarming, when the father may have expected some back talk from the teacher.

THIRD She didn't argue with the father when he insisted that Susan could read. She didn't wish to build a wall to impede progress as the interview moved along. It was too soon to point out facts. The father was not ready for them. Facts don't have much meaning when emotions are at a high pitch. The teacher was waiting for a better time.

FOURTH The teacher herself apparently felt that Susan's greatest problem was her not being accepted by the group. Although she probably knew that the child's lack of achievement was mainly due to somewhat limited intelligence, she still felt that the child could achieve more if she were happier. This, of course, was an approach that the father could accept more readily and was the one she chose to use. Perhaps, at another time, when the parents were more ready, there could be a discussion of the fact that Susan learned some things slowly. Now it was more important to help Susan, through this interview, to have more of a chance of being happy.

FIFTH The teacher made it clear that she was interested in the child and that she, too, felt badly that the little girl didn't seem to be happy and wasn't usually chosen by the others. The father ignored this at first, but, rightly or wrongly, she brought him to the point of accepting this as a possible factor in Susan's achievement. He was then ready to make a constructive step toward helping to improve the situation. It is possible that it was the teacher's kindly attitude and manifested interest in him and his child that helped bring the father around rather than just what she said.

SIXTH She ended the interview on a cordial note and left the door open for further communication. At no time did she show any annoyance over his unexpected appearance and initially belligerent attitude. Apparently this father was genuinely concerned about his child. His anger seemed to stem from his anxiety. Therefore the teacher accepted it and succeeded in helping the father view the situation in a better light.

Attempting to ascertain the problem

A parent may come to school of his own accord because of some smoldering resentment. Without time to obtain any background on the case, the teacher is handicapped in helping the parent to bring his problem out in the open.

Teachers should know that almost every teacher, at some time or another, has an unsuccessful interview with parents. Even the most skilled ones have a rugged time of it. No one can hit it 100 per cent. Sometimes it's the unfortunate things that the teacher says. Everyone says the wrong thing at one time or another. Sometimes, no matter how skillfully the teacher has conducted the interview, the desirable results are not obtained. Teachers must remember that sometimes when parents are seemingly extremely angry with them, actually they are only giving vent to feelings that may have had an entirely different source. Personal troubles at home, in which there is great emotional involvement, can sometimes bring a parent to school in a very angry state to discuss something quite foreign to the problem itself. Teachers should not, then, get disturbed unless they know that they have a real part in the blame.

It might be interesting to cite the following unsuccessful interview and attempt to see why it worked out as it did. In this case, the teacher had to seek the cause of the parent's resentment in the interview itself, since she had no time to find out about the home situation. The following excerpts are from an actual interview which a teacher wrote up and sent to us.

The child, Patsy, in the fifth grade, is average in intelligence, but about five months below grade level in reading. She understands arithmetical processes, but is very careless.

Her writing is satisfactory, but she seldom completes an assignment. She masters the spelling words for the week—if she is present that week. Patsy has no close friends; tends to be overbearing and bossy; seldom joins in games; likes square dancing. She seldom completes a task and wanders around the room. In appearance, the child is neat and clean. She is absent one-third of the time.

Like so many records, Patsy's cumulative record contains a preponderance of negative items, with few positive factors on which to build. Naturally the teacher does not have all these characteristics clearly in mind when, shortly before the noon hour at the large school, the mother opens the classroom door, walks in, and waits just inside the door. The teacher approaches her with a pleasant, questioning smile.

Mother: *Miss Gregg?*
Teacher: *Yes.*
Mother: *I've brought Patsy her lunch money and brought back her report card.* (Thrusts the card at the teacher angrily.) *This is the worst report card Patsy's ever had!*
Teacher (glancing back at the restless group of children): *Won't you come in and wait, Mrs. Franklin, until I excuse the children for lunch? I'll only be a minute or two—then we can talk. Feel free to look about the room, won't you?* (The teacher excuses the children for their lunch period. The mother stands stolidly, glaring at nothing in particular. After the teacher has given the money to Patsy and excused the children, she returns to the mother.) *Well, if we're lucky, nobody will come in for a ball or lunch that has been forgotten! Why don't we sit down at the library table?* (Both seat themselves.) *Here. I'll move these books aside.*
Mother: (No acknowledgment.)
Teacher: *It was Patsy's idea to put the water barrel and chicken coop on the covered wagons. They're well done, don't you think?*

Mother: *Humph!*

Teacher: *Let's see, Mrs. Franklin, you were wondering about . . .*

Mother: *The report card.*

Teacher: *Tell me, what part are you questioning most?*

Mother: *All of it!*

Teacher: *Do you understand how we grade? Perhaps you would like me to explain that first.*

Mother: (Looks down glumly.)

Teacher: *Well, the most important thing to understand is the fact that we mark according to the individual. Suppose there is a child with a high potential who is not working according to what he is capable of actually doing, even though working up to grade level. Well, he'd get an N, which means he needs to improve, or an S, which means satisfactory, at the very best— while a child who is not capable of doing grade-level work but who is working to the best of his ability is entitled to an E. You see, it depends on the child and the work he achieves in relation to his ability. It isn't just the results according to grade standards.*

Mother: (Says nothing.)

Teacher: *Is that a little clearer? It's just a little difficult to explain.*

Mother: *I understand.*

Teacher: *Now, which particular phase still puzzles you?*

Mother: (Says nothing.)

The teacher tries to discuss Patsy's out-of-school and home activities, her behavior in class, and possibly reasons for Patsy's not feeling at home in the class after she has been absent. She asks about Patsy's reported pains in her legs and her friendships. The teacher suggests that having some tasks at home might make Patsy feel that she is needed. To each of these approaches, the mother either says nothing or makes a noncommittal or uncooperative comment such as "I can't be there," "I don't know," or a brief negative statement. If the teacher had had more time to prepare for this interview, she might possibly have found some clues as to what was troubling or annoying the mother.

Teacher: *Why don't we both try to give her tasks to be responsible for?*
Mother: (Says nothing.)
Teacher: *Let's try that then, Mrs. Franklin, and I'll let you know how Patsy does in the near future. Shall I call or write you?*
Mother: (Says nothing.)
Teacher: *I'll write to you. All right? I'm sorry, Mrs. Franklin, but I have duty on the playground. Would you like to join me there?*
Mother (rising and walking to the door): *I have to leave.*
Teacher (opening door): *Let me tell you again how glad I am that you came. Please do come again, won't you?*
Mother: *I'll see.*
Teacher: *Good-bye, Mrs. Franklin.*
Mother: (Turns away without a word.)

This is the kind of interview that makes teachers lie awake nights! The teacher who reported this one was really quite worried about it and wondered what to do next. It happens that she is an excellent, conscientious teacher who has the best interests of her youngsters at heart and who usually does very well with her interviews. She actually knows the techniques of a good interview and started out bravely enough, despite the difficulty of greeting the mother while dismissing her class. However, the lack of response from the mother upset her somewhat, and, in her desperation, she became confused as to how to proceed. Let's see now what actually happened.

FIRST She was caught by surprise, in a rather awkward position, but she handled that well. She was cordial to the mother and tried to help her to be comfortable while she took care of her immediate duties.

SECOND She made a good attempt at establishing rapport, doing about all she could do. She complimented Patsy and showed what a contribution she had made to the mural, but still the mother would have no part of it. Directing attention to the mother—asking her why she was so upset about Patsy's report card—might have prompted more response.

THIRD Having done her best at establishing a relationship and knowing that she had failed, she thought she had best come to grips with the problem; so she asked the mother what phase of the report card she most objected to. The response "all of it" must have been a bit disheartening.

FOURTH Casting around for someplace to jump next and perhaps thinking that an explanation of the grading system would be helpful, she launched into that. Perhaps because she was somewhat flustered and also because what she had to explain was rather difficult, she did flounder a little and left out the point that she really wanted to make—that Patsy was capable of better work. (She got to this later in the discussion of attendance.)

FIFTH Still not getting any desirable response and remembering that one reason for an interview was to get and give information, she began to ask the mother questions about Patsy's home life. While this was quite an acceptable thing to do, she unconsciously put the mother on the defensive and probably increased her resentment; the teacher really lost ground rather than gained it.

SIXTH It might have been wiser for the teacher to give the mother a chance to give vent to her anger or simply wait in a relaxed way for the mother to try to tell what was bothering her. Once the mother had been relieved of her feelings, it might have been possible for them to begin to explore Patsy's progress and to come to some understanding. Maybe not. Teachers need to know that sometimes interviews are just plain unsuccessful because of the personalities and circumstances involved. We can only say that, in general, if the aforementioned guideposts for an interview are used, there is a better chance for a successful conference.

Clarifying a problem and finding a solution

Let's take a look at one more interview, this time exactly as the junior high school reported it, and find what we can see in it.

When parents take the initiative to come to school, they usually are very much concerned about something. To find out what the problem is, clarify it, and work out a solution is the task of the skillful teacher-interviewer. Sometimes as in the following interview with the mother of a junior high school girl, these purposes can be achieved successfully even under unfavorable conference conditions.

> This adolescent, Jean Hamilton, had not showered at all after her physical education class; consequently her grade had been lowered. Showering, or lack of showering, is considered in reporting achievement in physical education. When Jean's card went home, I commented that her lack of showering was the cause of her lowered grade. When the card was returned, her mother had written this comment: "I think this is silly. What has showering got to do with Jean's grade?"

> Two days later, Mrs. Hamilton came to school and Jean brought her into the physical education office. Jean introduced her mother to me, and then I asked Jean to go out and dress and go to her next class. Mrs. Hamilton asked, "Why is it so important that girls take showers?"

> I replied, "It's rather noisy in here right now, Mrs. Hamilton, with all the girls dressing. Perhaps you'd like to see our building and what Jean does in physical education. Then when the girls have gone out onto the field, I'm sure we'll be able to talk a little more easily. Otherwise, I'm afraid they will be interrupting us all the time."

> Mrs. Hamilton said, "Well, yes, I would like to see it. Jean has told me what a big place this is."

As we walked out into the locker room, I said, "This is our locker room. Each girl has a small locker issued to her to keep her gym clothes in and shares the adjacent big locker with five other girls during the course of the day. The showers are at the end of each of the five locker sections." Mrs. Hamilton nodded, but said nothing.

We went out into the hall and down to the big gym. I explained, "We share the big gym with the boys. We work out a schedule whereby we have the gym two or three days a week and the boys have it the other days. We play volleyball, basketball, and other games in here, and also dance and tumble."

"My, it is big, isn't it?" said Mrs. Hamilton. "And so clean. It hardly looks like the old gym I used to play in."

"Gyms have shown a lot of improvement over the years. They are much better lighted and have a little color, instead of the old drab tan and gray. We like our green gym." We went on through the gym to the smaller orthopedic gym, where I briefly explained our orthopedic and modified program. From there we went through the first-aid room and I opened the door to the cot room.

"This room is used by our modified classes—by students who must rest or who do not feel well enough to take part in physical education."

"You mean you let them come in here and lie down instead of going to class?" asked Mrs. Hamilton.

I replied with, "Only if they are not well enough to take part in some way—scoring, umpiring, or some such quiet job. Sometimes during their menstrual period they rest, or if they have been absent for several days with a cold or the flu—something that warrants rest rather than play." Just then the bell rang, so I said, "Now the locker room should be cleared, Mrs. Hamilton, if you'd care to return to the office. I think we'll be able to talk without any interruptions."

We walked through the hallway, as the stragglers dashed out to squad lines. As we entered the office, I offered Mrs. Hamilton a chair, sat down on the stool opposite her, and asked, "Did you notice our showers as we walked through the locker room?"

"Yes, I did, and it seems to me they are pretty open."

"Pretty open? I'm afraid I don't understand what you mean, Mrs. Hamilton," I replied.

"Well, heavens, everyone can watch you taking a shower" was her irritated reply.

"Oh, I see what you mean. Is that what Jean dislikes about showering here at school?"

"I don't know about Jean disliking it, although I wouldn't doubt but what that's it, but I don't think it's a good thing to have the girls undress and shower and so on, right there in the open—in front of everyone else. After all, I want my girl to develop a little sense of modesty."

"I agree with you about developing modesty in the girls. We like to think that all of the girls think along those lines."

Mrs. Hamilton's reply to this was "And how do you expect to develop such a thing if the girls are forced to undress and shower under the circumstances?"

"We have always felt that dressing with the other girls helped them to overcome a 'false modesty.' By that I mean, by dressing with the other girls around them, they soon develop a healthy attitude toward their own body and those of others. They begin to take physical differences as a matter-of-fact, everyday thing, and soon forget anything but undressing and dressing as quickly as they can so as not to be late to class. They do not have time to worry about the people around them, as their dressing time is rather short and they have to tend to business or they soon learn they will be tardy to this or their next class. I believe all of the girls are a little shy the first few weeks in the seventh grade, but they get over it quickly, as no great issue is made of it.

Dressing and showering are just an accepted part of their physical education class."

"Well, perhaps the changing into their gym clothes isn't so bad, Miss Boone, but this showering—all together, in a gang—I just can't see that."

"Yes, I guess if Jean is very modest, the group showers would bother her," I replied. "But perhaps there is something we can do to help her. If you'll step out here into the locker room, I'll show you what I have in mind." I took Mrs. Hamilton to the south end of the locker room, where we have several enclosed, private showers. Here I explained, "These showers are usually reserved for girls to use during their menstrual period, but I think we might find a solution to Jean's problem by allowing her to take her clothes out of her locker, bringing them down here after class, and showering in a private shower. Do you think Jean would agree to that?"

"As long as showering is part of her grade, I hate to see it suffer just because she is so bashful. I think this might be a good idea if you'd let her do it."

I replied, "I'd be glad to, if you think it would help. She can check her towel in just like the other girls, and then I will know she has taken a shower."

"Will you explain it to her, Miss Boone? I really don't think she objects to the shower itself—just to the idea of a group shower."

"Surely, Mrs. Hamilton, I'll be glad to tell her. I'll do it tomorrow during class, and perhaps you could also speak to her at home tonight. I think many of the girls feel that showering is just one of our rules—something we impose upon them just to inconvenience them. But really, it's a matter of health education. They play pretty hard, and most of them need a shower to remove the perspiration they have worked up. It's a matter of personal hygiene, and with so many of them being sweater-and-skirt fans, I think it's a little easier on the sweaters if they shower."

Mrs. Hamilton smiled and said, "I'd never thought of that. I'm forever having to send Jean's sweaters to the cleaners."

"Well, maybe this will help a little," I replied. "Jean seems to enjoy physical education. She plays well with the other girls, and she generally makes out well with her skill tests. Her coordination is very good. I was very sorry to have to lower her grade on account of her not showering. You see, she never told me the reason she objected to showering. I had no idea she was so shy."

"No, I don't suppose she would. She's awfully bashful. Sometimes her father and I worry about it."

"Well, this shyness sometimes goes along with the adolescent period. Perhaps she will outgrow it."

"I hope so."

"So do I, Mrs. Hamilton, and perhaps letting her use a private shower at the present time will help. Maybe in time she will want to return to the regular showers with the other girls. It sometimes happens, but we'll let her decide for herself."

"Thank you, Miss Boone. I surely do appreciate your understanding Jean's problem, and I'm sure she will. I won't take any more of your time. I know you are busy and have a class, but Jean came home very upset and I wanted to see about this showering business."

"Well, I hope you understand our point of view, Mrs. Hamilton, and I think I understand better now how Jean feels. I'm very pleased to have met you. Do feel free to drop in any time. I'll call you and let you know how Jean is getting along."

Here again we have a parent who came of her own accord because she was rather upset about a particular school regulation and did not understand the reason for a lowered grade. And here again was a teacher who, because she was interested in the student, was able to gain helpful information about the adolescent's feelings so that the whole situation might be corrected.

The teacher used good judgment in the way she handled this conference.

FIRST Because of all the confusion and noise at the moment, she took the mother out to see the new gym and explained the program to her, being careful to stay away from the problem of the grade and showering until an appropriate moment.

SECOND When the mother expressed her disapproval of the group showers, the teacher skillfully explained why they had that kind and later pointed out that for those girls who were too shy, they did have private showers.

THIRD Sensing that possibly Jean's showering problem stemmed from modesty, the teacher was quick to let the mother know that an adjustment could be made.

FOURTH She agreed to carry out the mother's suggestion that she talk to the girl about the situation.

FIFTH She closed the conference on a cordial note. The mother went away feeling friendly toward a department for which she had felt nothing but hostility before.

Parents come to school unexpectedly for various reasons and in various frames of mind. Some are dissatisfied with the way reading is taught. Some feel that the school is too free. Many are disturbed because their child is not getting as high marks as the parent wants. Some object to homework—too much or too little. Quite a few are concerned with the child's social development and his relationship with other children. There are also parents who want the teacher to know about an emergency in the family, to get help with a home problem, or to have the child excused for a trip the family wants to take.

Whatever the reasons, however, and whatever the attitudes, the wise teacher will do everything possible to accept the situation, unfavorable as it is, and concentrate on learning from the interview itself. He will make the conference with these parents beneficial to the child or adolescent and help the parent to understand the program better.

Conferences regarding reports of progress

CHAPTER SIX

The positive attitude   Meaningful mechanics   Guideposts to a successful conference   "Don't's" to avoid   Conditions affecting a child's progress   Clarification of parents' role   Attitude toward education   Parent-child relationship   Understanding the child   Acquaintance with the school program   Appreciation of the teacher   Progress impeded by family relations   Unrealistic parental aspirations

Parents are usually eager to know how they can promote the child's learning and are disturbed if they think he is making insufficient progress.

Parents respond in many ways to the report card or whatever form of progress report the child brings home. At one extreme, some parents punish him severely for a poor record. This punishment is often entirely undeserved; the child is doing the best he can. More common practice is to scold the child or deprive him of privileges—no playing after school, no TV, no parties—until the marks are improved. Children complain that their parents are never satisfied; that even when the report is good, they say, "You could have done better." The most understanding parents try to help the child in specific ways; they refer him to the teacher if they do not know how to help.

→The usual report card gives parents very little basis for helping the child do better. Even a letter is likely to be too general or too noncommittal to be of much help. In a conference with the parent, however, the teacher can discuss dated samples of the child's work and uncover sources of difficulty; together, parent and teacher can assume definite responsibilities for helping the child. Probably the most significant trend today in reporting pupil progress is the increasing emphasis on parent-teacher conferences.

Conferences with parents may make a teacher very nervous. This is especially true of the new and inexperienced teacher, but even many experienced teachers view parent conferences with some trepidation. This is quite natural, for a teacher always feels just a little on the spot with parents of her pupils. After all, she feels that she is being judged by them and that her reputation depends considerably on their opinion of her. Even though the teacher may be apprehensive about an interview, however, there are many things she can do to alleviate her fears.

The positive attitude

First of all, she needs to realize that she has it in her power to help each child by talking to his parents. She needs to feel that the responsibility of helping the child to his best growth is a shared thing, that the parent is eager to learn from her and also eager to work out whatever is best for the child. When she invites the parent to come for an interview, the teacher should not feel that the parent will come in a critical attitude. The teacher herself should never enter into a conference with a negative or critical attitude. She must remember that the main purpose of the conference is to share thinking, information, and planning which will benefit the youngster; therefore a positive attitude is essential. It will help considerably to allay fears of facing the parents of any child. The conference should be looked upon as a friendly meeting—an opportunity for two or more adults interested in the same person to sit down and have an informal but constructive and purposeful talk.

Meaningful mechanics

In order to feel more secure about conducting the interview, the teacher should make some preparation for it. She needs to have several things in mind and certain specific materials at hand before entering into the conference. Planning such details as the following is particularly helpful:

1. Clarity as to the main purpose of the interview; i.e., giving information and getting information about the child; giving an accurate appraisal of his work; learning possible causes for his behavior, good or bad; planning with the parent for his best possible growth; and interpreting the school program to the parent.
2. Having the classroom in an acceptable condition, fairly orderly but with adequate, meaningful materials in evidence—just as any classroom should be at any time. The appearance of a classroom tells quite a story to the most casual observer.
3. Several examples of the child's work at hand so that the teacher can use them as concrete examples as she gives her appraisal of the child to the parent.
4. The child's cumulative record. From this, the teacher can interpret to the parent the trend that the child's progress has taken. Naturally the IQ, usually recorded in such a folder, would not be revealed to the parent.
5. The child's report card. The teacher needs to be very certain of just what each grade given implies and why she gave that grade to the child. She might have to justify some of the grades; not to be able to would be most embarrassing.
6. Knowledge of the child's actual ability and his achievement in relation to it. The wise teacher will be able to

judge from what the parent reveals about the home situation and attitudes of expectancy toward the child whether to suggest more or less pressure for the child's best progress.

7. A pretty good estimate of the child's strengths and weaknesses in regard to his social adjustment, ability to get along with other children, attitudes toward adults, and the like.

8. Arrangement of a fairly comfortable physical setup for the interview. It is usually unwise to have the parent sit across the desk from the teacher because the parent might easily get a nostalgic feeling of a teacher-pupil relationship from bygone days or even a sense of employer-employee relationship. Any essence of formality detracts from the potential of a good conference. Other physical arrangements, such as seating the parent where she will not have to face the glare or suffer from a draft, should be a consideration of the teacher.

Guideposts to a successful conference

With such careful preparation, then, for the interview, the teacher should feel considerably more adequate to carry on a successful conference. All of the above-mentioned suggestions are easy enough to work out, but what to do when the parent actually arrives requires planning of a different kind, since the teacher cannot possibly know what will be said or what direction the conference might take. It is obviously impossible for us to present a recipe for a good interview and guarantee that, if it is used, a teacher can be assured of success. However, a few guideposts and some concrete examples of recorded interviews may be of some help to the reader.

FIRST The note home, inviting the parent to come to school, should be very friendly and informal. It should make clear to the parents that the teacher is interested in their child and that the conference is for the purpose of making things better for him. A note should never contain anything which could conceivably put the parents on the defensive or bring them to the conference in a hostile mood. It must bring the parent to the school as a friend of the teacher, who is a friend of theirs and of their child.

SECOND When the parents arrive, the teacher should greet them in a friendly, gracious manner, putting them at ease as quickly as possible. An expression of appreciation of their coming and other cordial remarks are quite in order. It is essential that a good feeling be established before the interview really gets under way.

THIRD In getting into the conference, the teacher should make some very positive remarks about the child of these parents, relating some specific incident to illustrate them. A humorous anecdote often gets things off to a good start. Most certainly an expression, on the part of the teacher, of her interest in the child helps considerably to establish a good rapport.

FOURTH In addition to making the positive remarks about the child, as a person, it is important for the teacher to begin her remarks about his work from a positive angle, pointing up his strengths before indicating where he needs most to improve. In this way she keeps the parents with her and can move into the more doubtful areas with a little more assurance of their cooperation and good feeling. Naturally, some discussions will be about children at the bottom of the class and seemingly achieving nothing. To talk with their parents is a difficult thing for the teacher, but, even so, surely these children have done something of merit, whether in subject matter or human relationships. The teacher must have something good to say about them, with specific examples to back it up.

FIFTH As the teacher talks of the academic achievements of the child, she should show the parents some of his paper work and then indicate how she has arrived at his rating on the report card. As she shows the written work, she has an excellent opportunity to indicate the methods used in teaching the particular subjects and of interpreting the program. Many parents are skeptical of the modern methods of teaching, but if the teacher will take this opportunity of explaining why we use these methods and how they actually work, she can help the parents to be much better satisfied and to become better friends of the school.

SIXTH The teacher must not be afraid to indicate the areas in which the child needs to improve. If it is a subject-matter area in which he is weak, she should show how she is attempting to help him to improve and what the parents might do to help him at home. If it is a behavior problem which needs to have some attention, she should not be afraid to explain the problem. But she must do this in a kindly, positive way, being very careful not to put blame of any kind on the parents. She should let the parents know that she is seeking their help and enlightenment on the matter and should help them to feel that this problem should be a shared responsibility in which she is most happy to do her part. The child should never be made out to be a little monster but rather an immature person who needs additional guidance and help to work out the specific problem he presents.

SEVENTH The teacher must make a conscious effort throughout the interview to *listen*. Parents often have good ideas and are much more likely to be willing to carry *them* out than those a teacher might impose on them. The teacher should encourage the parents to express their ideas, including suggestions she might follow to improve the child's school report.

The teacher should be willing to listen, too, if the parents wish to voice their criticism. Some parents will be highly critical, but if the teacher is able to accept their feelings without becoming defensive or argumentative, she will be able to make more progress with them in the long run. Arguing merely puts up a wall which does more harm than good. Progress is rarely made through arguments or defensive statements. It is ever so much better to accept the criticism, letting the parents get things off their chests and *then* gradually and quietly getting around to interpreting the kind of thing which will help them to understand the "why" of the program and the "why" of the methods used. Remember that the parents' point of view is based on their own experience. And never forget how important the child and his achievement are to those parents. The teacher is interested in the child, to be sure, but that interest cannot possibly compare with the interest the parents have. The teacher must realize, then, that any criticisms that parents express are emotionally tied up in this tremendous interest.

EIGHTH In concluding the interview, the teacher should summarize the conference rather briefly, again indicating the child's strengths, where he needs to improve, and what she and the parents can do to help him to improve in all phases of his growth. These should be concrete specifics that are really possible.

NINTH The teacher should again indicate her appreciation of the parents' visit and invite them to drop in whenever they can find a convenient time. She should also let them know that she is willing to send home a note from time to time if necessary to indicate lack of progress or outstanding progress.

"Don't's" to avoid

During an interview the teacher should keep in mind a few rather important "don't's":

1. Don't put the parent on the defensive about anything.
2. Don't talk about other children or compare this child with other children. It is most unprofessional.
3. Don't talk about other teachers to the parents unless the remarks are of a complimentary nature.
4. Don't belittle the administration or make derogatory remarks about the school district.
5. Don't argue with the parent.
6. Don't try to outtalk a parent.
7. Don't interrupt the parent to make your own point.
8. Don't go too far with a parent who is not ready and able to understand your purpose.
9. Don't ask the parents personal questions which might be embarrassing to them. Only information pertinent

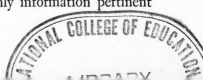

to the child's welfare is important. Questions asked out of mere curiosity are unforgivable.

10. After the conference don't repeat any confidential information which the parent may volunteer. It is most unprofessional and can be very damaging to the parent or the child.

Conditions affecting a child's progress

When the child begins school, parents usually show a great deal of interest in his progress. They attend PTA meetings and welcome the opportunity to talk with the child's teachers. There is much that they can do to help the child get off to a good start and facilitate his continued learning during the elementary school years. Some of the following conditions affecting the child's progress often come up in the parent-teacher conference with this focus.

Clarification of parents' role

Both teachers and parents need a clearer conception of the parents' role during the elementary school years. This is a prerequisite for successful parent-teacher conferences.

Some parents are too eager to teach; they want to take over the teacher's responsibility. They are very ambitious for their child. On the assumption that one cannot have too much of a good thing, they ask: If instruction in school is desirable, why not have more of it at home? Perhaps they have been reading a book that described the magic method of learning.

An overzealous attitude on the part of parents has a number of possible disadvantages. "All work and no play makes Jack a dull boy." He becomes tired of the tension of formal learning. He resents not being allowed to play with the other children. If he does not learn as quickly as his parents expect him to, he senses their impatience. If he is a sensitive child, he may become anxious about losing his parents' love. Moreover, if parents are too much concerned about school success, the child may feel that his parents care only that he be a credit to them.

If the teacher uses one method and the parent another, the child may become confused. Even if the difference in method does not bother the child, he may find himself siding with the teacher against the parent, and this may disturb him.

If there is some underlying hostility between the parent and the child, it may be transferred to the learning situation; it may even color the child's attitude toward learning in general. Efforts to teach a child at home are complicated by many social and emotional factors. Some of these might have to be recognized in the parent-teacher conference.

Fortunately, it is seldom necessary for the teacher to say "Don't" in parent conferences; there are many positive ways in which parents can contribute to a child's success in elementary school.

Attitude toward education

The parents' attitude toward education affects the child's interest and effort. Most middle- and upper-class families give the education of their children top priority. When the child comes home from school, they ask him what he has learned. One first-grade teacher made it a practice to discuss with her pupils at the end of each day what they had learned. Thus they were primed for their parents' questions. One day the teacher neglected to do this. When one parent asked, "What did you learn in school today?" the child replied, "Teacher didn't tell us." By showing an interest in the child's education, parents increase his sense of the importance of his school tasks.

Children whose parents show indifference toward their efforts often have the feeling that nobody cares whether they learn or not. In fact, some children are discouraged from learning. If they come home speaking correct English, they may be told that they are putting on airs. If they sit down to do their homework, they are distracted by people coming and going, by demands that they run errands or do chores, or by the blare of television or radio.

Moreover, there may be nothing in the parents' daily activities that shows any recognition of the importance of education. They do no serious reading and show little interest in any cultural activities. If the child identifies closely with his parents, their example affects his attitude toward school learning even more than their words.

In parent-teacher conferences, parents often reveal their individual attitudes toward education. Although it may not be possible to change the parents' habits and attitudes, the teacher may persuade them to take greater pride in the child's school achievement or to provide him with home conditions that are more conducive to learning.

Parent-child relationship

We have repeatedly emphasized the importance of the parent-child relationship. This relationship is equally important to the child's learning during the elementary school years. A father can keep a child's love even though he is firm and strict and even punishes the child, as long as the child senses that the parent loves him and is all for him. Under these conditions, strictness is conducive to achievement.

Understanding the child

It is equally important to understand the child and to want him to develop in accord with his nature and capacity. If the child is an able learner, the parents should recognize his ability; they should neither exploit and overstimulate the child, nor deny him opportunities to develop his potentialities. To this end, the parents should study child development and make use of his daily observations. The school people should be glad to supply additional specific information.

The parent conference furnishes the ideal situation for imparting information. In the opinion of the writers, it is unwise to allow parents access to the school's cumulative personnel records; the information on them is too susceptible of misinterpretation. In the parent conference, the teacher can select the information he thinks the parents will use wisely and explain its significance with respect to the individual child.

There is an art in interpreting and synthesizing personnel data. Each item is a fact or opinion from which a number of inferences may be drawn. No important decisions should be based on the results of a single test. No conclusion should be final. The child is growing and changing. New facts about him and new observations of his behavior require a continuous revision of earlier impressions. Something of this approach to the understanding of a child may be conveyed to the parent by a teacher who has this attitude toward child study.

Acquaintance with the school program

When parents understand what the school is trying to do, they can cooperate more effectively. When a parent complains about the "progressive methods" a teacher uses, he may have little understanding of what the teacher is attempting. Teachers should share their philosophy of education with parents. By explaining why Janie has not yet begun to read from a book in the first grade or why Bert does not have homework of a formal nature in the fourth grade, they help the parent to provide the home experiences that will supplement and reinforce school instruction.

By forestalling a parent's criticism of the school, the teacher is helping the child, too. No good can come of destroying a child's faith in his teacher or his confidence in the teacher's ability to help him learn.

General information about the school can be given more efficiently by means other than the parent conference. Parents may be invited to the child's class, to open-school night, or to meetings in which the school program is described.

Appreciation of the teacher

Teachers are human; they appreciate approval. With them, as with children, praise is more effective than blame. A word of commendation stimulates them to make greater efforts in behalf of the child.

The parents' attitude toward the teacher is likely to be caught by the child. The more the child respects the teacher, the more he will profit by her instruction. If the child is having difficulty in learning arithmetic, for example, it is helpful if the parent knows that the teacher is using the best modern methods. This reinforces the child's feeling that learning arithmetic is not an impossible task. With the teacher's help it can be done.

The parent-teacher conference should promote mutual appreciation. The parent gains an understanding of the teacher's problems, and the teacher becomes more sympathetic toward the parent. Their good relationship increases the child's confidence in both home and school.

Progress impeded by family relations

Keeping in mind the guideposts of a good parent interview and also keeping in mind some of the don't's, let us turn to a recorded interview between a teacher and the mother of Tom. The teacher has provided some background information. It becomes clear upon reading this that she felt the need for a conference with the mother, both because some of Tom's schoolwork was not good and because he seemed to be having difficulty with his peers. Here, then, is the case of Tom.

Tom is 6½ years old and is in the first grade. He has average intelligence and a little better than average physical ability. He is not reading as well as he could. His independent work is spasmodic, sometimes completed and well done and sometimes unfinished and poorly done. The teacher has talked to Tom about why we do good work and has praised his good efforts repeatedly.

He has trouble getting along with his peers, on the playground especially. He seems to lash out at others, kicking and hitting when a game doesn't go to please him or when he feels he should have a turn. He will also throw a tantrum—screaming, hitting, and kicking—for no apparent reason except to get his own way. The teacher has noted that on the days his work is poor in the room, he has more trouble outside, too.

Tom and the teacher have had several private conferences about this behavior and why it isn't acceptable to kick and hit. He is very reasonable and ready to admit he has done wrong. He is sorry and apologizes and sincerely promises to think first the next time. During the second of these talks with Tom, the teacher asked him a few questions about his home life. She found that he had a two-year-old sister, that his father was gone most of the time, that his mother was always busy with the baby and that she no longer read to him as she used to. The teacher asked Tom whether he helped his mother a lot; he replied that his mother didn't have time to let him help. The teacher felt that a parent conference might be helpful, and so she telephoned Tom's mother one day when he was absent. The following telephone conversation ensued:

Mother: *Hello.*

Teacher: *Hello. This is Mrs. Mead, Tom's teacher. I was wondering if he was sick.*

Mother: *Yes, a little, I guess. He complained of an upset stomach this morning and he was running a little fever, so I kept him at home. Nothing came of the upset stomach, and he seems to be feeling much better this afternoon. I think he'll be back at school tomorrow.*

Teacher: *That's fine. I'm glad he's feeling better, and we'll be happy to have him back at school tomorrow. I also wanted to ask if it would be all right with you if Tom stayed after school a few minutes each day and watered the plants for us.*

Mother: *Oh, yes! That's perfectly all right, if you're sure he won't be in your way. How is Tom doing in school? I've been thinking that I should come over to school to see how he's doing, since we haven't lived in this area very long. But my little girl keeps me pretty busy and my husband isn't home very much, so it's rather hard for me to get away.*

Teacher: *I know it must be difficult, but it would be fine if you could come over for a visit soon. I like to get acquainted with the parents of my children as early in the year as possible. I'm free any afternoon after 2:30, but if you'd like to come during the school day, that would be fine, too.*

Mother: *No. After 2:30 would be fine. Maybe I could come next week. Could I let you know?*

Teacher: *Yes, certainly. Just send a note with Tom, telling me what day, and I'll be expecting you.*

Surely this mother would be coming in a cooperative mood, wouldn't she? An invitation, by telephone, can often set the stage very nicely. Here the teacher also took advantage of a natural opening to call the mother. It doesn't always happen that there is a natural opening, but teachers should be alert to such if they are feeling the need for a parent interview. Now, let's see how the actual interview itself went.

Teacher: *You're Mrs. Pike, aren't you? Please come in. I'm Mrs. Mead, Tom's teacher.*

Mother: *Yes, I'm Tom's mother. I'm very glad to meet you.*

Teacher: *Won't you sit down? I think you'll find that chair fairly comfortable.*

Mother: *Oh, yes, this will be fine.*

Teacher: *I'm so glad you were able to come this afternoon, Mrs. Pike.*

Mother: *To tell you the truth, I almost wasn't able to come; then Tom acted as though he didn't want me to come, and I began to think that maybe he wasn't getting along too well and that I should come and talk to you. It was so nice of you to telephone the other day.*

Teacher: *I generally try to phone when a child is absent, although I usually don't get it done the first day. But I wanted to talk to you and get your permission to let Tom stay after school to help us.*

Mother: *If you really want him to stay, he surely may. I'm usually pretty busy about three o'clock anyway, as Margie is waking up from her nap about that time. Her daddy will have the job of getting her dressed today.*

Teacher: *Oh, yes, Tom told me that he had a baby sister. How old is she?*

Mother: *Oh, she is almost two years old, and she really is a doll; but she surely does take a lot of my time. She has blonde hair and blue eyes; not like Tom. I don't know how come. My husband and I are both dark. My husband finally got home yesterday—for the first time in about three weeks. He's a contact man for the refrigerator company, and he has to do a lot of traveling.*

Teacher: *I suppose Tom misses his father when he's gone so much. In fact, I suppose you all do.*

Mother: *Yes, I surely do miss him, but I really should be used to it by now. He's been doing this sort of work for several years now. I suppose Tom does miss his father, although he never says much about him when he's gone.*

Teacher: *I have some of Tom's work here I thought you'd like to see. Here are several nicely done papers. He can do such very fine work; we are most proud of him.*

Mother: *Those are really very well done for a six-year-old, aren't they? I didn't know he could do such good work. He has brought some papers home but, as I said, I'm usually pretty busy about the time he gets home and I don't get a chance to see them. What about these two papers?* (The teacher had put two poor papers at the bottom.) *He didn't do nearly as neat work on these, did he? Didn't he have enough time to do them?*

Teacher: *Yes, he had the same amount of time for these papers as he had for the others, but for some reason he didn't do as good a job on these. I was wondering whether you had any idea why sometimes he does poor work when he can do such nice work?*

Mother: *No—unless it would be the days when he's in one of his rebellious moods—at least that's what I call them. Some days he just seems out of tune with everything and everybody.*

Teacher: *That's interesting. What do you mean by "out of tune"?*

Mother: *Oh, he's just impossible. He won't leave the baby alone. He picks her up and pushes her down, and I'm just afraid he'll hurt her. I have to watch him every minute. When I punish him, he screams and kicks or sometimes sulks and won't eat. I suppose when he has a day like that, his schoolwork won't be done right either.*

Teacher: *That may very well explain why some days he does poor work. Also on those days he seems to have difficulty getting along with the rest of the children. Have you any idea why he feels this way?*

Mother: *No, I really don't. I took him to a doctor and had a physical check-up before he started school last fall. The doctor said he was just fine physically. He really seems to like school. I had quite a time to keep him home that one day last week. You said he doesn't get along too well with the other children. What does he do?*

Teacher: *Much the same as you said he does at home. He pushes the others around, and he also kicks and hits when things don't go his way. He's always sorry afterward and apologizes sincerely.*

Mother: *I didn't realize he was behaving this way at school.*

I just can't understand why he should act this way. He used to be the sweetest child, and he never gave me any trouble at all when he was younger.

Teacher: *When did you first notice these unhappy days?*

Mother: *Oh, about the time he started kindergarten. No, it was before that, I guess. Of course, I was so busy with the baby that I didn't pay too much attention at first. Let's see, Tom didn't act this way before the baby was born. I remember now, because I had to stay off my feet, and he and I used to play games together. I also used to read to him quite a lot. It was one way of entertaining him and keeping him quiet so that I didn't have to go chasing after him.*

Teacher: *I imagine Tom really enjoyed having you read to him and play games with him. Does he still enjoy it?*

Mother: *I don't really do it any more. Since the baby came I'm so busy with her . . . (pause). You don't suppose that's what's bothering him, do you? I don't read to him any more. He has asked me to several times, but he always seems to ask when I'm the busiest. You know how that is.*

Teacher: *I surely do. But maybe Tom is actually trying to get your attention by acting up the way he does sometimes.*

Mother: *Well, he does get my attention when he pushes the baby down and screams or pouts. But that's not the kind of attention he should have, is it?*

Teacher: *No, I guess it really isn't.*

Mother: *But I just don't know when I'd find time to sit down and play games with him or read to him as I used to.*

Teacher: *Does Tom have any jobs to do at home? Maybe he could work with you. Then he'd be getting your attention by doing something to help you.*

Mother: *No. It's generally easier for me to do things myself, but I suppose there are some things he could help me with. He could help me make his bed in the morning. I suppose he could wipe the dishes for me, although when my husband is gone, there aren't too many.*

Teacher: *Those are very good ideas. And I think giving Tom special jobs like that, to help you, would make him feel important to you.*

Mother: *Yes. I can see that I really haven't given Tom any special attention lately. After I get the baby in bed at night, I'll just simply sit down and read Tom a story or play a game with him. He used to have lots of fun playing little games with me. I really enjoyed playing with him, too.*

Teacher: *I'm sure you both had fun, because Tom does think things through when he isn't upset, and he also has some original ideas to contribute to our group discussions. He has taken quite an interest in the plants. I never have to remind him to water them. In fact, I'm afraid they might be getting a little too much water. Would you like to see them?*

Mother: *I surely would.* (Mother and teacher spend a short time discussing the plants.) *Oh my! I didn't realize how fast the time had gone. I surely hope I didn't take too much of your time, Mrs. Mead.*

Teacher: *No, you didn't at all. I'm so happy you could come, and I do hope you can come back soon. Perhaps you could come in the morning and hear Tom read. His group reads from about 10:00 to 10:30.*

Mother: *I'd like to. Do you suppose Tom would like it if I came to hear him read?*

Teacher: *I think he would. Most first graders like to have their parents come to school. First grade is pretty important to them.*

Mother: *Yes, it is, isn't it? I do hope Tom will get along better in school. I'm certainly going to have him help me do some things at home. My, it's been nice to talk to you.*

Teacher: *I have enjoyed talking to you, too, and I do hope you can come back again soon. Good-bye, Mrs. Pike.*

Mother: *Good-bye, Mrs. Mead. I'll try to get back soon to hear Tom read.*

Let's review this interview and see why it was successful.

FIRST   As we have already noted, the teacher used a natural opening for the telephone call and let the mother know how interested she was in Tom. She quickly followed up on the mother's comment that the latter thought she would like to visit the school. Then, when the mother arrived, she was most warm and cordial in her greeting.

SECOND   She made the mother as physically comfortable as possible and established an easy, informal atmosphere.

THIRD   Before getting into the business at hand, she let the mother talk a bit about things near and dear and interesting to her.

FOURTH   She was probably wise to show the mother the good work that Tom had done first so that when the poor work came to light, the mother would raise the natural question. This gave a nice lead into why his work should be sometimes good and sometimes poor.

FIFTH   She led the mother into seeking the answer. ("I was wondering whether you had any idea why sometimes he does poor work when he can do such nice work.") The teacher didn't try to impose her thinking but sought that of the mother. We can be sure that the teacher already had a pretty good hunch, in her own mind, where some of Tom's difficulty lay, but she was most careful not to place blame anywhere.

SIXTH   She continued to ask the kind of question which would help the mother to pursue the problem, and she was most sympathetic whenever the mother seemed to be blaming herself for what she hadn't been doing, at the same time tactfully indicating that she was sure that Tom would enjoy doing those things which were all-important to him, i.e., having his mother read to him, etc.

SEVENTH   She made a good suggestion about how Tom could get the right kind of attention from his mother. This was done in such a natural way that it would seem that the mother could take it and use it most easily.

EIGHTH   It will be noticed that the mother did most of the talking while the teacher listened attentively, picking up and making the most of any suggestion the mother had. ("Those are very good ideas. And I think giving Tom special jobs like that, to help you, would make him feel important to you.")

NINTH The teacher didn't attempt to get into Tom's achievement very much, feeling, probably, that if Tom got more attention at home, he would have more good days, when his work was always quite acceptable. She would probably want to have a follow-up interview in the not-too-distant future, when she could get into this a little more thoroughly. She made a good start in helping to relieve Tom's difficulty. She should not try to cover too much at any one time. However, if she had felt that the mother might not come again or that she wouldn't have time to see her again very soon, she might have done a bit more about evaluating Tom's progress and even told the mother more about the things they did in the first grade. In general, it is better to deal thoroughly with one or two ideas than to attempt to cover too much. Too many ideas, while they may seem simple and familiar to the teacher, may result in confusion to the parent, who perhaps may not be sufficiently oriented to organize them in her mind to use them.

TENTH The teacher left the mother with a nice feeling of some pride in Tom's extra work on the flowers. Too, she left the door open for the mother to come again whenever she could, making her feel that she was most welcome.

Unrealistic parental aspirations

Let's take a look at still another interview now—this time at the high school—and see whether we can get a sense of how interviews should go. Later we shall deal with some in which the parent has not been in such a cooperative mood.

Mr. Briggs, teacher of first-year algebra, had become quite interested in David, a pleasant, cooperative, but rather withdrawn boy who simply seemed unable to grasp algebra. He was concerned about the boy because he noticed that he was by himself almost all the time, apparently having no particular friends. Because he was concerned about the boy as a person and because of David's lack of success in the algebra class, Mr. Briggs decided to see what he could find out about the boy. He examined his cumulative folder and found that in the fifth grade his IQ had been recorded as 96 and at the seventh grade as 101. His arithmetic grade-placement score at the seventh month of the eighth grade was 8.3, some four months below the norm. Almost all his grades had been average, with the exception of two courses in shop, in which he had received A's. Comments on the record indicated that the teachers felt he could do better if he would only assert himself. A counselor's comment read, "Parents very ambitious for the boy. Insist on academic program before trial in more general course."

Mr. Briggs then had a brief conference with the counselor to see whether he had any further information. The counselor said that when he had programmed the boy, he had suggested that he take general mathematics before going into algebra. The boy had agreed to that, but upon taking a copy of his program home, had met with considerable disapproval from his parents, who accompanied him to school the next day. The father said that the boy was to be an engineer and that he needed to get right at the preparatory math without wasting a whole year fooling around in some little old arithmetic course. The counselor had pointed out that the boy was not very strong in math and that perhaps, in the long run, more time would be saved by strengthening the fundamentals. The father would not hear of it, however, and so the boy was placed in algebra. The counselor had the impression that this boy was very much dominated at home and that the parents were very ambitious for him. They themselves were college graduates.

Both Mr. Briggs and the counselor thought that perhaps the boy's tendency toward withdrawal stemmed from a feeling of inadequacy as a result of his inability to live up to the expectations of his parents. They decided that it would be wise to have a conference with the parents, if the boy agreed to it, to see whether they might not take some of the heat off him. It was agreed that Mr. Briggs would ask the boy to come in during his conference period.

Mr. Briggs: *David, this algebra is kind of rough for you, isn't it? Is that why you don't like it?*

David: *I don't know. I just don't understand it. I got lost about the second week.*

Mr. Briggs: *Several people did. It's a pretty rugged course unless you have quite a knack for math. Did you like math in elementary school?*

David: *Not too well. I mostly made C's and C minus in it. The counselor didn't think I should take algebra, but my folks made me. I guess I'm failing, huh?*

Mr. Briggs: *Well, Dave, I'm surely not going to flunk you, because I know that you've been trying, but I just don't think that you ought to continue it next semester. Lots of students drop this and geometry, foreign languages, and other things after the first semester because they find that it just isn't for them. You're probably very good in other things.*

David: *I'm not so hot in anything but shop.*

Mr. Briggs: *You like shop? What would you think about taking that shop-math course next semester? It's a practical course and especially slanted toward helping shop students.*

David: *I'd like to, but I know my folks won't let me. They'll make me go on with this. I don't know what they'll say if I don't make it in here. They want me to be an engineer.*

Mr. Briggs: *That requires an awful lot of math and science, David. Maybe you're not quite ready to tackle the preengineering course yet. Maybe it would be better for you to try a semester of the shop-math and see how that goes. Then, possibly, if it seems right, you could try algebra again. What would you think about my talking to your folks about that?*

David: *It would suit me. But I don't think my folks will go for it.*

Mr. Briggs: *Shall I ask them to come down?*

David: O.K.

Mr. Briggs is faced with quite a problem, but it is one of the most common problems that teachers and counselors have to meet. Let's see how far he gets. He isn't too hopeful as he pens a note to David's parents:

Dear Mr. and Mrs. Wright:

I am very much interested in your son David. He's one of the nicest chaps that I have in any of my classes. He's most cooperative and is working very hard in algebra. However, he's finding it pretty difficult, and I'm wondering if perhaps you and I might not get together to see how we can help him to work out this problem. My conference period is from 2:15 to 3:10. Could you come down to see me then? If not, I will be available after school here or I would be glad to come to your house. Please let me know if you would care to have a conference and what the most convenient time would be. I am looking forward to meeting you.

Sincerely,

M. N. Briggs

Mr. and Mrs. Wright, who were most interested in their boy, made an appointment just two days later. They arrived at Mr. Briggs's classroom in a rather anxious state of mind.

Mr. Briggs: *You're Mr. and Mrs. Wright, aren't you? Come in, won't you? I'm Mr. Briggs.*

Mr. and Mrs. Wright: *How do you do.*

Mr. Briggs: *Shall we sit over here? I have nothing but the students' chairs to offer you, but maybe that will make you nostalgic for the good old days.*

Mr. Wright: *I don't know. It was so long ago that I was in a classroom that I can hardly remember what it was like. My wife and I graduated from Stanford almost twenty-five years ago. Our oldest boy finishes there next year. He's going on in engineering. And, of course, we want Davy to do that, too. What's all this about his having trouble in algebra? Isn't he working? I'll see that he spends more time on it. I make him study it an hour every night now. I knew it was a little hard for him in the beginning; so I tried to help him study, but he got so upset I had to quit. Practically cried—big kid like that, too. Well, he knows he has to get it because he's going to be an engineer. There's a big demand for engineers. Fine thing for a young man to go into these days.*

Mr. Briggs: *Yes, it is—and I can understand your concern about David's getting his algebra. Engineering requires a tremendous amount of math and science all right. But David is finding it pretty difficult, and it isn't because he doesn't study. He's trying very hard and he's a most cooperative boy. You really should be very happy to have a son like Dave.*

Mr. Wright: *Well, I'm not going to be happy to have a son who isn't getting his work. I tell you I'll make him spend two hours a night if I have to.*

Mr. Briggs: *Well, I'm not sure that an extra amount of time is going to solve this problem, Mr. Wright. His skills are not too bad, but he's like a lot of people who have trouble with algebra; he just isn't able to comprehend the processes. It's a very difficult subject, you know, and few people really master it. He doesn't seem to have the knack of getting at it. I think maybe he isn't ready for it.*

Mr. Wright: *But he has to be ready for it. He has to get it out of the way so he can get at the other courses.*

Mr. Briggs: *Yes. I can see how you feel about that, but if the boy isn't ready for it and can't get it—and, really, I know Dave is trying—then there is no use in our pushing it at this time. He doesn't have any self-confidence at all, and I wonder a little if this doesn't have something to do with his achievement. Would you know why he lacks confidence?*

Mr. Wright: *No, I don't. We've always told him that we knew he could get good grades if he tried and that we knew he could go to college if he worked hard. Certainly we've made him feel that we have lots of confidence in him. I don't see why he wouldn't have it in himself.*

Mr. Briggs: *Do you think that he might be afraid that he couldn't live up to your expectations? He seems to admire you so much that it might be bothering him to feel he isn't coming through for you. Sometimes those feelings keep a youngster from being able to achieve all he could. Self-confidence is pretty important to all of us.*

Mrs. Wright: *Yes. That's true, but I've never thought about David's lacking self-confidence.*

Mr. Briggs: *How does David feel toward his elder brother? Are they close?*

Mrs. Wright: *Oh, David has always looked up to Taylor. And we try to spur him on to work harder by pointing out what Taylor has done because we know that David would like to be like Taylor.*

Mr. Briggs: *Yes, I can see how you would do that. Do you think that maybe David thinks he could never do as well as Taylor?*

Mr. Wright: *Well, I've never thought much about it. Of course, David has never been as good a student as Taylor, but I always figured it was because he didn't try as hard. He never seemed to be as interested in studying. Always wanted to fool around with the car and mechanical things. Taylor isn't so interested in the manual things; he enjoys the theory more.*

Mr. Briggs: *It's possible that they have different kinds of minds and different interests. From what I can gather, David is very skilled in mechanics and practical things. Again, however, he may feel quite inadequate because he hasn't measured up to Taylor in the more academic type of thing. David is really such a fine boy. I wonder if we aren't expecting a little more of him than he is able to produce right at this time. He's pretty young yet. What would you think about encouraging him to do the things he is capable of doing right now and praising him for his successes in them? Perhaps we could build his confidence up to the point where he could achieve more academically. Perhaps not. It's possible that David will never be adept at this kind of math. Your other boy is. But everyone has different talents and interests. David may want his own garage some day. If he does, you and I may be going to him to borrow money, huh?*

Mr. Wright: *Maybe so. I hadn't thought about his lacking confidence. And maybe we have been pushing him pretty hard. I want him to go to college though, and so he has to get this stuff. If he doesn't get it now, he'll just have to get it later. Are you thinking he should drop algebra now?*

Mr. Briggs: *Well, not right this minute, but it would probably be wise for him to drop it at the end of the semester and pick up another kind of math course. Since he's so interested in mechanics, it might be wise for him to pick up the shop-math course. We can see how he makes out in that. In the meantime, since he enjoys his shopwork so much, maybe we can all show a lot of interest in what he does there. It might help his ego out a little and give him a little more feeling of adequacy in other things as well as shop. What do you think?*

Mr. Wright: *Well, I guess that's all right. Worth a try anyway. Appreciate the interest you've shown in our boy. I'll want him to have you for algebra next year.*

Mr. Briggs: *If it seems right for him to have it, you can be sure I wouldn't let any other teacher have him. It was good of you both to come over to school. I know you're a busy man, Mr. Wright. Good-bye, Mrs. Wright. Come again any time.*

Let's take a good look at this conference now and see what Mr. Briggs did.

FIRST He made it very clear that he was interested in David, first to the boy himself, in the very kindly way he talked to him about his difficulty with algebra, trying hard not to let David feel singled out as the only one having difficulty.

SECOND He made it very clear to the parents that he was interested in their boy and considered him a really fine chap, even though algebra was not exactly his forte.

THIRD He didn't argue with Mr. Wright about David's ultimately taking algebra, but very tactfully suggested a lack of self-confidence as being the probable reason for lack of accomplishment.

FOURTH He didn't blame the parents for David's lack of confidence but merely asked casual, tactful questions which would help direct the father's thinking on this matter.

FIFTH He realized that this parent was not ready, at this point, to accept the fact that David would probably not be able to get recommended grades in math; he avoided expressing his own opinion. Rather, it was a matter of planting a little seed of an idea so that at a later time the matter might be pursued, depending, of course, on David's success the next semester.

SIXTH Again and again he assured Mr. Wright that he understood the importance of his ambitions for his son; he was careful not to argue or to contradict anything the father said.

SEVENTH He made it clear several times how much he thought of the boy and that he was concerned about his welfare.

EIGHTH He closed the interview on a friendly, constructive note.

Mr. Briggs was fully aware, during the whole interview, of the ambitions of this father for his son—ambitions that weren't quite realistic perhaps. He was also aware that much of David's difficulty might be due to too much pressure and too great expectations, but never once did he give straight advice or give the father information which he couldn't handle. He merely guided the father's thinking. It is hoped that ultimately Mr. Wright will recognize the individual differences between his two sons and appreciate David's interests and talents as much as he does Taylor's.

Conferences
with parents
of preschool children

CHAPTER SEVEN

Conditions conducive to preschool children's development   Knowledge
needed   Preschool as a prelude   A common concern

"If only Joan's parents had been more affectionate to her as a
baby or small child, I don't think she would be so demanding of
attention now," Joan's fourth-grade teacher said.

"If only Johnny's parents, during his preschool years, had
spent more time reading aloud to him, talking with him, and
listening to him telling them about the exciting things he had
seen and heard and handled, I think he would have got off to a
better start in reading in school," his first-grade teacher thought.

"If only Sally's mother had found some playmates for her
or sent her to nursery school when she was four or five, perhaps
she wouldn't be so shy now and find it so hard to relate to other
children," her third-grade teacher remarked.

"*If only*"—so many times teachers in elementary and even
in high school feel this way. They believe that some of the
social, emotional, and academic problems which children are
having in their classes might have been prevented if parents had
only realized the importance of infancy and the preschool years
in children's development. Some undesirable tendencies, some

personality fault lines could have been prevented or deflected if parents had only known.

Conditions conducive to preschool children's development

At each stage of their development children need parents. During their infancy, their parents can give them a sense of trust, a feeling that all's right with their small personal world. The later preschool period is the time when children form attitudes that determine their approach to learning experiences. Prior to school entrance, parents can help children acquire specific knowledge and skills that create readiness for reading and other school learning.

To be sure, a parent-teacher conference cannot change any parent's deep-seated attitudes or basic personality structure, but it may help the parents to change their behavior in minor ways that may have a major beneficial effect. The parent's behavior may lead to an improvement in the child's behavior to which the parent will naturally respond more favorably. Thus, a beneficent circular response is set in motion.

Despite shifts in theories about bringing up children, between fluctuations of emphasis on control and permissiveness, there are certain attitudes and parent behavior that teachers can safely sanction. No one has denied the importance of genuine love for the child, though love is not enough. In infancy we would approve unconditional love. This is the time, as a well-known psychiatrist said, for children to be bad and parents to be good. It is the time to build a basic sense of trust. Later, during the preschool years, children have to learn that they share the responsibility for maintaining this loving relationship. The patience of the most loving parent has limits, and children must learn when their behavior is out of bounds.

Parents have to be careful not to play favorites. If possible, they should treat each child with equal affection. Sometimes they will tell the teacher how much they are sacrificing for a handicapped child in the family. Such sacrifice is not good for the handicapped child or for other children in the family. Jealousy of a brother or sister is sometimes a distracting influence in school; it usurps attention the child should be giving to the mastery of his school subjects.

Inconsistency in discipline seems to have more unfavorable effects than either overstrict or overlax discipline. Not knowing definitely what is expected of him, the child cannot form standards of right conduct. When parents disagree, the child may become still more confused.

Parents sometimes demand too little of a child. "He's so small," they say, "and childhood should be happy." True; childhood should be happy, but overcoming difficulties and having a sense of accomplishment is one of the greatest sources of happiness for both children and adults. Emerson once said that we need "somebody who shall make us do what we can." If the task is suitable for the child's stage of development, there is usually no reason why the parent should not expect him to do it at the proper time. Unless the preschool child learns to accept and fulfill suitable responsibilities, he is not likely to adjust well to the more rigorous requirements of the school situation.

From the earliest years, parents can contribute to the child's success in reading. Reading aloud to him interests the child in books and acquaints him with the language patterns of literature. Seeing parents and older brothers and sisters reading for information and enjoyment increases his desire to learn to read. As he builds up his speaking vocabulary, through talking and listening, he is increasing his reading readiness. Learning to distinguish sounds and shapes is only one step removed from associating letter sounds with letter symbols in beginning reading.

These are some of the conditions conducive to child development that teachers should keep in mind when talking with parents of preschool children. If the teacher is able to reinforce any of these favorable responses on the part of the parent, it is all to the good.

Knowledge needed

If the teacher has some idea of the development that can be expected of preschool children of a certain age, he can ask more
significant questions in the parent-teacher conference, such as:
How does he play with other children? How well does he listen
to a story? Is he curious and eager? How does he show these
characteristics? What kind of directions can he follow? Is he
negative and aggressive at times, or has he got over this stage?
If he has had an interesting experience, how well can he share
it with others?

The mother of a preschool child has much to contribute to
the teacher's understanding of the family situation, pointing out
some temporary or chronic trouble, such as:

Illness of some member of the family
Unemployment of father
A new job that takes the father away from home a good
  deal
Attitude of other children in the family toward the pre-
  school child (tease him, baby him, hit him, etc.)
A hospital experience the child has had
Jealousy of a younger brother or sister

A general open-end question at the beginning invites the mother
to bring up any questions, problems, or satisfactions she would
like to discuss with the teacher. Sometimes these are family
problems which contribute little or no help in understanding the
child and cannot be discussed in the limited time available.

Preschool as a prelude

That the early years are crucial for the development of attitudes
and a central core of personality has long been recognized. Some
writers have gone so far as to say that a child's personality is

determined during the first two years of life. After that, they say, he tends to make each new experience conform to his preconceived ideas.

We cannot accept this doctrine of the early determination of personality; we have seen many people continue to change all through life. A famous guidance study at the University of California, conducted by Dr. Jean Walker Macfarlane, found that predictions made about adolescents had not, in many cases, come true fifteen years later.

The possibility of later change, however, does not minimize the importance of the preschool years. During these years the child forms attitudes toward himself and other people and toward work and play. He develops either a sense of trust or a feeling of apprehension about his world and the people in it. He becomes either self-reliant and reasonably independent *or* lacking in initiative and overdependent. His insatiable curiosity about everything he sees and hears and handles is encouraged *or* suppressed. It is clear to any teacher that the attitudes and modes of behavior that the child brings to school have much to do with his school success or failure.

Many pamphlets have been prepared by school systems, educational organizations, and commercial publishers for parents who have children about to enter school, but printed material is not a substitute for personal contacts. There is still a need for group meetings and conferences between teachers and parents of preschool children. There are occasional meetings with parents of preschool children and perhaps a conference with the first-grade teacher the semester before the child enters kindergarten or first grade. But this is too late. Predispositions that may affect later school performance often have their roots in infancy and early preschool years.

In these days of large families, school-age children often have brothers or sisters of preschool age. It is therefore possible for teachers to include in their regular conferences with parents of children in their grade some discussion of the preschool children in the family, as in the following instance:

Teacher: *Janet tells me she has a baby brother, a four-year-old sister Betty, and two brothers, eight and ten. Girls at Janet's age often feel motherly toward little children.*

Mother: *Yes, she does seem to like them and never has much trouble in making them mind.*

Teacher: *You've done a very good job in bringing up Janet. She's one of my best readers and gets along well with her classmates. Are you bringing up your other children in the same way?*

Mother: *Well, I'm working now and don't have as much time to give to the baby and the four-year-old as I did to Janet.*

Teacher: *How do you manage? . . .*

As the mother describes her efforts to meet the needs of all the children, she is reassured about the good things she is doing and sees more clearly the family group in which each member has some responsibility. In discussing the importance of the preschool years as a prelude to the child's school success, the teacher has an opportunity to voice her approval of the favorable features of the preschool child's program as the mother describes it, to suggest a few improvements, and to refer her to several of the best available pamphlets. A word to the wise parent in the parent-teacher conference may have an effect on the preschool child's development quite disproportionate to the time spent.

A common concern

Many mothers will ask the teacher for reading exercises and drills to prepare their preschool child for beginning reading. In such instances the teacher should tactfully suggest that results are usually better in the long run when the child takes the initiative for his own learning and the parent follows the child's lead. If he wants to know what this sign says or what this word means, if he is interested in the sounds of words and the shapes of letters, by all means tell him. Give him interesting experiences to talk about, listen to him, read to him, and encourage his curiosity and self-learning. All this is sounder preparation for beginning reading than formal exercises and drills which may bore him and make him dislike reading. Information of this kind is frequently given in the teacher's conference with mothers of preschool children.

One such conference proceeded as follows, after the parent and the teacher had discussed Joanne, who was in the teacher's second-grade class:

Teacher: *You have a preschool child, too, haven't you?*

Mrs. B.: *Yes, Janie's three now.*

Teacher: *Joanne was very well prepared for first-grade work. Are you giving Janie similar experiences?*

Mrs. B.: *Well, we read aloud to both children, to Janie during the day when Joanne is in school, and before bedtime their daddy reads to both children some poem or story that we all enjoy.*

Teacher: *Reading aloud is important. It gives children a good feeling toward books and acquaints them with the vocabulary and language patterns of literature.*

Mrs. B.: *We've always talked a great deal with the children, too. They have breakfast and other meals with us, and we try not to be too busy to listen to things they want to tell us.*

Teacher: *I noticed that in the "Show and Tell Period" Joanne was very good at telling us about interesting things she had seen and done.*

Mrs. B. (laughing): *I imagine the children give you much information about their home life!*

Teacher (laughing): *Yes, as they see it. Sometimes I tell parents I'll not believe all the children tell me about their parents if they will agree not to believe all that the children say about their teacher! I imagine both your children have many books at home and constantly see people reading for different purposes.*

Mrs. B.: *I wanted to ask you about the best books for both children.*

Teacher: *Probably Janie has already had the linen picture*

books and is old enough now to learn to handle books carefully as she would a pet. When you and her father are looking through a magazine, you can sometimes let her turn the pages and look at the pictures. Soon she will enjoy the many beautiful picture books now published for preschool children. She will soon enjoy going to the library with you and Joanne.

Mrs. B.: *I'll plan to take them more regularly to the children's room in the library. Joanne likes to choose her own books, now that she can read beginner's books.*

Teacher: *That's fine. Reading many easy, interesting books is the best way to make her a fluent reader, ready for more challenging books as she grows older.*

Mrs. B.: *I never tried to teach Joanne to read before she came to school. If she wanted to know a word, of course I told her, and she learned the names of the letters from her ABC blocks and books. When she pointed to a letter as she played with them, I'd tell her the letter name. She also liked to "read" pictures.*

Teacher: *That was helpful. Anything of this kind, done in the game spirit, is useful. It prepares children to recognize the sounds and shapes of letters and words when they begin reading instruction in school. . . .*

Mrs. B.: *Are there certain things I can do to prepare Janie for her school experience?*

Teacher: *You are doing many things, Mrs. B. In many ways you're encouraging her natural curiosity and desire to learn. You let her look at and listen to and play with many kinds of things, take her on little trips, listen to the things she wants to tell you, speak clearly and correctly to her, answer her questions, read aloud to her, and give her the impression that books and reading are a delight. All this in a balanced schedule of sleep and rest, good eating habits, and outdoor play, both alone and with other children, is just about ideal.*

Mrs. B.: *What about TV?*

Teacher: *I guess TV is part of the modern world. It is bound to command some of her attention.*

Mrs. B.: *It's not a problem yet with either child. They are content to look at one or two children's programs a day. I think they like being read to better than looking at TV.*

Teacher: *There's no substitute for the personal contact between parent and child. That's a great advantage that reading aloud has over television. Television is so impersonal.*

Mrs. B.: *I'm glad Joanne is getting along nicely and thanks, too, for taking time to talk about Janie.*

In this interview, the teacher's main contribution was to reinforce the best features of the mother's present practice with her children. This was important; a confident parent is more effective than an indecisive, anxious parent. There is always something that can be commended. Occasionally there is a parent who seems to do and say all the wrong things, and yet has no harmful effect on the child; this is because underneath the surface behavior there is a genuinely loving parent-child relationship. Where this quality exists, specific suggestions from the teacher are likely to be accepted and applied. The most difficult interview is the one with a parent who knows all the right answers but does not really love the child.

Both child-care practices that encourage independence and parental approval for achievement seem to motivate children to do well in school. However, we should consider the possible danger of developing children who are so intent on personal success that they forget to be kind.

Teachers can safely reassure parents who feel guilty about the mistakes they have made, or are worried about the opportunities they lost in earlier years, that no single mistake or omission is fatal; individuals change throughout life as they face such critical events as vocational decisions, marriage, and the birth of children. Every aspect of an individual's development is the result of many causes.

Since the preschool years are so important for the child's later success, school people cannot afford to neglect this period. Books and pamphlets are helpful. They should be supplemented and implemented by group meetings of parents. Individual conferences with parents of preschool children are most helpful of all; they should contribute greatly to the better adjustment of children after they enter school.

Conferences
with parents
about
reading problems

CHAPTER EIGHT

Background knowledge of reading Prereading experiences Reinforcement during elementary school years *Clarification followed by suggestions* Discussions of phonics The "spur fallacy" The need to be challenged *Ideas to emphasize*

One of the topics most frequently discussed in parent-teacher conferences is the child's reading. This is quite understandable because of the importance reading holds in our culture. Parents expect children to learn to read in the first grade. When the child doesn't bring home a book early in the first grade, parents want to know why. If he reads slowly and haltingly in the second grade, they tend to become impatient with him. If he is behind the other children in reading at the end of the third grade, they are greatly concerned. When serious reading retardation makes itself evident in the intermediate grades, they seek remedial help. If reading-test results in the sixth grade show that he is one or two years below his age or grade placement, they wonder whether he will be able to meet the increased reading demands of high school. In the junior or senior year at high school, both parents and children wonder whether a speed-reading course might not contribute to success in college. These are only a few of the reading problems that crop up in parent-teacher conferences.

Background knowledge of reading

The more the teacher knows about reading the better. There are many home experiences that reinforce a child's school learning. From parent-teacher conferences and group meetings parents may gain insights and suggestions that supplement their own common-sense efforts to help their child with his schoolwork. To be able to discuss these opportunities with the parents, every teacher should be aware of the contribution the home can make to a child's success in reading, during both preschool and school years.

Prereading experiences

In addition to general attitudes, the preschool child may acquire specific learnings that facilitate his progress in school. His prereading experiences pave the way to success or failure in beginning reading. Children from privileged homes, who have been read to, who have had many opportunities to see interesting things and talk about them, who have learned to distinguish different sounds and shapes, who know the names of the letters of the alphabet, and who have had other experiences that make them eager to read, are ready to learn when they enter the first grade. On the other hand, children from bilingual or underprivileged homes are usually not ready to begin systematic reading instruction until these prereading experiences have been supplied in school. A summer kindergarten is very helpful for these children.

...

Reinforcement during elementary school years

Throughout the elementary school period parents should continue to provide new experiences, encourage conversation, take interest in the child's progress, and show affection for him. When a first grader says, "Mommy, let me read to you," Mother becomes an appreciative audience. When a child who has learned important word-recognition skills hesitates over an unfamiliar word in his reading, the parent encourages him to use his newly acquired skills to puzzle out its meaning. When a fourth-grade child asks a searching question, the parent may say, "Let's see whether we can find out." When a seventh grader's interest in voluntary reading is temporarily sabotaged by the comic-book craze, the parents find books for him that have the same appealing qualities of action, adventure, suspense, and mystery. When a child of any age becomes lazy, the parent tries to find out why.

Clarification followed by suggestions

Teachers should be acquainted with the popular articles parents are reading. Through these articles and certain books—some of them as persuasive as they are unsound—many parents have become convinced that their child's reading problems are due to lack of phonics.

Discussions of phonics

Conversations like the following frequently occur in parent-teacher conferences:

Mother of a ten-year-old boy who is not able to read second-grade books fluently: *My husband and I both think Dick's reading difficulty is due to lack of phonics. He was taught in the beginning just to recognize the words as a whole.*

Teacher: *Has he had instruction in phonics since that time?*

Mother: *Oh, yes, we've had a special tutor who did nothing but teach him phonics.*

Teacher: *The special tests given by the psychologist show that Dick is very good at associating the sounds of words with letters. He has no difficulty in distinguishing different letter sounds and can recognize all the letters of the alphabet easily.*

Mother: *But his reading in the fourth grade is very poor. It's really painful to hear him read.*

Teacher: *Yes, he tries to sound out every word, even the small common words that he should recognize instantly at sight.*

Mother: *Yes, I've noticed that and also that he doesn't seem to be concerned with the meaning of what he reads. He tries to get out of reading every chance he gets.*

Teacher: *That's an important observation. We find these tendencies common with children when there has been over-emphasis on phonics.*

Mother: *But what shall we do now?*

Teacher: *I will introduce as much reading as possible that has personal meaning for him—directions he has to carry out, things he wants to know about. I'll also try to find interesting books on a level at which he can read fluently.*

Mother: *But that would be a very low level—first or second grade. I wouldn't want him to read books like that, so far below his age.*

Teacher: *You mustn't be embarrassed about his reading easy books or let him feel embarrassed. This is the best possible way for him to build up the basic sight vocabulary—220 little words that make up about 75 per cent of the running words in the books he will be reading. He should not have to stop and puzzle out these words.*

Mother: *Is there anything I can do at home?*

Teacher: *If he likes to play games, you could get him some of the Dolch word games, published by the Garrard Press in Champaign, Illinois. They will give him further practice on the basic vocabulary, but they are not a substitute for easy, interest-*

ing reading. He has to learn that reading has meaning for him and that reading can be fun.

Mother: *What about phonics?*

Teacher: *His knowledge of phonics will come in handy, too. When he comes to an unfamiliar word, we shouldn't usually tell him what it is, but encourage him to use his word-recognition skills, of which phonics is only one, to get the meaning himself.*

Mother: *You've helped me a great deal in understanding Dick's reading problem.*

Teacher: *By working together, I'm sure we can help him read up to his ability.*

This interview shows that the mother, having been convinced of the importance of phonics, stressed it so much that her purpose in making Dick a better reader was defeated. He was low-average in ability and may have started formal reading instruction before he was able to profit by it. The intensive tutoring in phonics gave him skill in sounding out words, but apparently diverted his attention from getting the meaning of what he read and created a dislike for reading.

The teacher was able to make these facts clear to the intelligent mother and to work out with her a sound program for the improvement of Dick's reading.

The "spur fallacy"

Parents also commonly complain that their children are not being challenged. They think the child should be given books of greater difficulty. This has been called the "spur fallacy." To give a retarded reader books beyond his present ability too often intensifies his feeling of inadequacy and inferiority, which is a major cause of his slow improvement in reading.

The following excerpt is from a conference with a parent who expected too much:

Mother of David, seven years old and in the second grade, who is below average in intelligence: *I was very much surprised when David brought home a book that was clearly labeled* Beginner's Book.

Teacher: *How did David feel about it?*

Mother: *Well, it was a funny book and he enjoyed it, but I said, "You should be reading second-grade books, not beginner's books."*

Teacher: *We all read easy books at times—even comic strips. Why shouldn't children, too, be allowed to enjoy easy books?*

Mother: *But David needs to be challenged by difficult tasks. He tends to be lazy.*

Teacher: *What happens when you give David one of those challenging books?*

Mother: *To tell you the truth, it usually ends in a scene. He begins trying to read, becomes restless, then gives up unless I stand right over him.*

Teacher: *I see. He doesn't get much satisfaction or pleasure from it. I wonder whether that has something to do with his attitude toward reading. He's becoming very anxious about reading and gives up as though he were sure he would not succeed.*

Mother: *That's just the way he behaves at home.*

Teacher: *As long as he has this attitude, he cannot put forth the effort reading demands. Don't you think we should try to change this attitude?*

Mother: *But how?*

Teacher: *By giving him the experience of getting pleasure and satisfaction from reading.*

Mother: *Letting him read those beginner's books he seems to enjoy?*

Teacher: *Exactly, and lots of others on the same level of difficulty. After he has developed fluency on that level, then we can very gradually give him somewhat more difficult material— books that have a few unfamiliar words that he is able to puzzle out, using the word-recognition skills he is now learning.*

In this parent conference, the teacher tried to point out the advantages of starting a child where he is in reading and moving ahead slowly as he gains fluency on the lower levels. One short conference, of course, cannot convince an ambitious mother of the difference between challenging and pressuring a child beyond his ability. However, David's mother seemed to accept the teacher's suggestion as reasonable and welcomed the list of books the teacher thought would be suitable for David's voluntary reading.

Without arguing with the mother, the teacher managed to present the facts convincingly as both she and the mother observed them. By directing the mother's attention to how David felt, the teacher hoped to divert her from focusing entirely on her own ambitions for him.

The need to be challenged

Quite a different type of conference is one in which the teacher, baffled by a bright child's slow progress in reading, hopes to obtain from the parent some clues as to the cause of the child's reading difficulty. The following interview is of such a kind:

Mother: *You said you'd like to see me about Teddy. I'd be only too glad to answer any questions you want to ask.*

Teacher: *Just tell me a little about his difficulty as you see it.*

Mother: *He just can't seem to master reading, though I'm sure he is a normal child. He makes nice friends, and I let him have his friends in to meals. Last year when I didn't let him play away from home, the other boys called him "Baby." I told him to drop friends who treated him like that, but he cried and said they were his friends, so I let him keep them.*

Teacher: *Have you done anything at home to help him improve his reading?*

Mother: *His father and I tried to teach him at home, but*

we could not help becoming impatient and he became restless and inattentive; so we stopped. I don't approve of the methods they used in school. My husband doesn't either.

Teacher: *Will you tell me more about that?*

Mother: *Well, it was a progressive school. They thought he wasn't ready for reading. He seems to be able to read a little now in the second grade, which he repeated, but he can't repeat what he's read. He seems to be trying hard. I really don't know what to do. Perhaps the accident he had may have something to do with it.*

Teacher: *What was the accident?*

Mother: *It was an auto accident in which his head was cut. We've had X rays and they say he's all right. He has no eye or hearing defects.*

Teacher: *That's important to know.*

Mother: *When my father lived with us for a number of years, he spoiled Teddy. Anything the child wanted, my father would get for him or do for him.*

Teacher: *So he never learned to do anything that was hard?*

Mother: *That's it exactly.*

Teacher: *Does Teddy have other lessons at home?*

Mother: *He takes music lessons, but it's hard to get him to practice. He does it very badly if I leave him alone.*

Teacher: *Do you leave him alone much?*

Mother: *No, I gave up everything and stayed home with him until he went to school. No one I could get was competent to take care of him. He's the only child we have, and we waited a long time for him.*

Although nothing conclusive about Teddy's reading problem came out in this conference, the teacher did get the impression that Teddy was an overprotected child. She thought possibly his immaturity in reading might be part of a general immaturity. At least, it would do no harm to give him more opportunity to take initiative and to pair him off for practice with one of his good friends who was an able reader.

Parents and teachers can be mutually helpful in dealing with children's reading development. This is common ground, with which both teachers and parents are vitally concerned.

Ideas to emphasize

In a conference on the role of the parent in reading and in other aspects of a child's school success, the teacher's aim is to help the parents become less dependent on the voice of authority— less eager to be told what to do and more independent and competent in judging what is best for their child.

In the course of the conversation, as opportunity offers, the teacher might introduce the following ideas:

Parents are not the only influence in a child's life. Other persons in the home—brothers and sisters, grandparents, and other relatives, friends of the family—have different kinds and degrees of influence. The school, the church, the neighborhood, and the world as it is brought into the home by radio and television, all have a bearing on the child's development. As the child grows older, the peer group exercises a greater control over his behavior. Although we do not know exactly what influence each of these factors exerts on the child's life, we should recognize that all of them may affect his personality and character. Both parents are needed. Each has a share in the total development of the child, including his development in and through reading.

Conferences
with parents
of the gifted

CHAPTER NINE

*Emphases in the guidance of the gifted   The school's responsibility
Aims in interviewing   Interview with parents of a gifted achiever
Interview with parents of an underachiever*

Within our gifted children lies one of America's greatest natural resources. This resource is the potential intelligent leadership which our country needs so urgently and which, in the past, has been relatively untapped and many times shamefully wasted.

Parents and school people face a challenge now as they never have before to identify and to set free the inner resources—the abilities—of these gifted children. Development of the potential power inherent in the keen minds of these youngsters is as vital as the development of any other natural resource of our country. For its very existence today, America cannot do less than to develop, utilize, and conserve this wealth which may lie locked in many of our children on all economic levels.

Emphases in the guidance of the gifted

Parents and schools have a common responsibility in nurturing the gifted child. The need for love and the security which comes from love and affection is as great for gifted children as for others. To function up to capacity, a child needs to feel that he is loved and wanted by his parents. With such security, he is in a much better position to be generous in his feelings toward other people; this, in itself, can help others to feel more acceptant of him.

Parents of the gifted child should be careful to help him to develop and keep a good perspective on his place in life. It is right that the gifted child know that he has certain responsibilities to society because of his potential. He should recognize also that his acceptance and understanding of people are important as well. He should learn to appreciate the contributions of less able people and to use his own powers to give leadership and ideas to those people, setting them free to contribute more than they otherwise would.

However, if a child is told that he is much brighter than other children and if he is given the idea that he is better than they are, his consequent attitude of superiority may make his potential followers turn from him to someone who accepts and appreciates them.

The school's responsibility

Many schools have been developing programs to help the gifted children to realize their potentialities. Test results are studied to identify the youngsters who have made outstanding scores. These scores are compared with the child's actual achievement in school. If the child is not achieving up to capacity, the school attempts to help him determine the cause and to remedy the situation. Sometimes it is a matter of selecting materials that appeal to the child's interest. Sometimes it means helping the youngster to adjust his sights toward a more appropriate goal. Often a conference with the parents helps to correct misunderstanding and to relieve tensions that have kept the child from putting forth his best efforts. Whatever the cause of underachievement, then, it is essential to investigate and to attempt to work out a solution.

Whether one of these gifted youngsters is achieving up to capacity or whether he is an underachiever, the parents and the school people should get together to share information and ideas which would benefit him. Teachers and counselors are sometimes in a quandary as to what to say in their interviews with parents of bright children. They feel that the parent should be aware of the child's potential; yet they don't want the parents to treat him as an infant prodigy. Too, they are anxious that the parents not leave a conference with grandiose ideas which, through parental pride, they would want to tell their neighbors. They want them to realize that while the child has high potential mental ability, he may be socially handicapped unless he is helped to appreciate other people and their contributions.

Aims in interviewing

It might be helpful for school people to keep the following points in mind as they interview the parents of a gifted child:

1. Establish good rapport. Indicate pleasure at meeting parents of such an able youngster.
2. Let parents know that the child seems to have high potential ability and that you want to talk to them about him—that you feel it would be helpful to share information, etc.
   a. Ask what the child is like at home.
   b. Indicate specific skills which he has demonstrated.
3. Discuss the responsibility that this child must learn to carry because of our need for the kind of leadership which he is able to give in one way or another.
4. Make clear to the parent that the child's ability is *potential* and that its development depends a great deal on the guidance he gets at home and at school.

5. Indicate that children with superior ability usually can be expected to share responsibility for their conduct at an earlier age than other children.
6. Point out the fact that these children will be in heterogeneous groups, where they should not act superior to others.
7. Stress the value of good human relationships and appreciation of the superior qualities of other children.
8. Give parents a list of books and periodicals which would be of real interest to the child for reading at home.
9. Indicate importance of the child's having a variety of experiences, such as visiting museums, zoos, factories, etc., talking to people in various kinds of occupations— experiences with some tasks which are not in the realm of his superiority.
10. Emphasize the importance of opportunities for creativeness at school and at home, such as painting, writing for children's magazines, hobbies, etc.
11. Be sure to let the parents know that you feel the future of this child is a shared responsibility of the school, the parents, *and* the child himself and that the school is anxious to do its part in providing stimulating and challenging experiences.

Interview with parents of a gifted achiever

The above-mentioned points are illustrated in excerpts from two interviews—the first with parents of a gifted child who is achieving up to capacity and the other with parents of a gifted child who is underachieving.

Belmont High School has a policy of interviewing the parents of all their gifted children. The record of this interview was sent to us by the counselor who, together with the science teacher, met with Terry's parents. The science teacher was the one chosen to sit in on the interview because of Terry's keen interest in that subject. He did well in his other subjects too, but in science he was most outstanding.

Terry was a nice-appearing boy, always neat and clean, but not particularly well dressed. He had an IQ of 135, on the Otis Beta, and scores on his achievement tests, given in his freshman year, ranged well into the twelfth-grade level. He didn't mix with the other students very much, though he did seem to have one good friend who also was a gifted student. His hobby was rigging up electrical displays which he could control through a central switch.

After the counselor and the teacher had greeted Terry's parents cordially in the counselor's office, the interview went on somewhat as follows:

Parents: *Terry isn't in any trouble, is he?*

Counselor: *Indeed not! I'm afraid parents often think that when we invite them to school, their youngster is in some kind of trouble. Matter of fact, it's just the opposite with your lad. . . . Mr. Hannah here can tell you what an outstanding student he is in science.*

Mr. Hannah: *Yes, I certainly can. It's been a long time since I have had such an able student in my class.*

Father: *Yes, he's interested in science. He's always talking about electricity and fooling around with it at home.*

Mr. Hannah: *I hope that he will continue his interest in science and go on with it.*

Father: *Well, that would be nice, but I'm afraid he'll have to go to work as soon as he finishes high school. We couldn't possibly send him to college.*

Counselor: *College is a pretty expensive proposition. I'd hate to have one of my children ready to go right now. But sometimes, with these able students who are genuinely interested in going on to college, there are ways to get help for them. I'm sure you know that various colleges offer scholarships. These don't cover all the expenses, but they help a lot. And the youngsters can always work on the side to supplement the scholarship money. We have several of our graduates doing that successfully right now. . . . We don't want students to feel that just because they have been blessed with a good mind, everything should be handed to them on a silver platter. They have definite responsibilities.*

Mother: *I agree with you. We've known, because of his grades and all, that Terry did well at school. But we've never thought of him as being outstandingly bright. And the idea of a scholarship has never occurred to us. If it should be possible for him to get a scholarship, we certainly would be happy for him to go to college and partly work his way through.*

Teacher: *You would be interested in having him go, then, would you, if he continues to do well and does manage to get a scholarship?*

Father: *Yes, if he could do that, it would be fine. It's just that we wouldn't be able to help him. We have two other children, you know, and it's tough these days to make both ends meet.*

Counselor: *Yes, we certainly appreciate that. And one child in a family should not be given advantages to the detriment of the other children. Of course, naturally, at this time we can't promise anything, but if Terry continues the way he is doing now, he should stand a pretty good chance.*

Father: *Uh, you feel our boy is pretty smart, huh?*

Counselor: *Well, he's proved to be an able student so far, and there's no reason why he shouldn't continue to be. We most surely can say to you that Terry is making the most of his potential ability in his studies. We'd like to see him use it a little more socially. He keeps pretty much to himself, you know, and we feel that he has quite a bit to offer the others. . . . Do you suppose we could encourage him to share both his interest and his activities with others more? How about in class, Mr. Hannah? Could you plan it so that he's working with and helping several others on some special project or something?*

Teacher: *Yes, I think I could. It might get him a little more interested in the other students as well as helping them to learn something too. . . . I could ask Terry to tell the class a little bit about the gadget he's rigging up at home. And then after he's described it, ask him if he'd be willing to show it to some of the class members. But how would you people feel about having a bunch of kids in your back yard?*

Parents: *Might not be too bad. . . .*

Father: *Should we make him study more? If he's pretty smart, shouldn't he be doing more than he's doing?*

Counselor: *He's working pretty hard, sir. I don't think he needs to be pushed any more on the study angle, but if all of us can do something to help him be more comfortable with people and to contribute to them, I think we probably ought to.*

Mother: *Maybe you're right. He does study hard, and I'd like to see him get out and have more fun with young people. And, Roy, don't you be going around telling people that Terry is smart. You'll have everybody hating you and the boy too.*

Father: *Uh.*

Counselor: *It's hard not to brag about a boy like Terry, but your wife has a point. Kids are funny. They have a tendency to resent an "average-raiser," as they call them. So it's probably best if other kids aren't aware that Terry is such a good student. Of course, they know that he does well, but perhaps the less said about it the better. . . .*

Counselor (in summary): *I will talk to him about the scholarship possibility. And if you have any ideas for us at any time, I hope you will let us know. In the meantime, we'll all be working toward the same end—to keep this boy at a high level of achievement in his studies and to help him to develop more interest in people.*

How well did the counselor and the teacher handle this interview? We might briefly review the interview as a whole.

FIRST They were cordial to the parents and indicated their real interest in the boy.

SECOND They quickly pointed out that they were eager to talk to the parents of such an able youngster, and the science teacher remarked that the boy was one of the most able students he had had in a long time.

THIRD Never once did the counselor or teacher use the term "gifted" or "very superior," but rather they said that here was a boy with potential who, at that moment, was using it.

FOURTH They gave good information to the parents about the possibility of the youngster's continuing his education; they were most sympathetic and understanding about the parents' inability to help out financially. Often parents feel badly because of their inability, but because of the way this was handled, they seemed to be quite comfortable and acceptant of the idea of the scholarship and of the boy's working.

FIFTH The important business of helping the boy to learn to enjoy and appreciate people was introduced quite easily and so handled that the parents felt a share in the plan for helping him.

SIXTH The counselor accepted the father's feeling of pride in the boy, saying that it would be hard not to brag about him, but he wisely reinforced the mother's idea that it would be a little rough on the youngster if others got the idea that Terry was a brain or a square. It is most important to accept the feelings of parents. Sometimes it helps them to express them at the school so that their need is not so great after they are out among their friends and relatives.

SEVENTH The conference was ended on a cordial note— that of reassuring the parents of the school's continued interest in the boy and in the plan of investigating the scholarship possibility.

This interview was not a difficult one to conduct, since the parents were exceptionally cooperative and the boy didn't present any serious problem. He was working up to capacity, and he did have at least one friend. With the cooperation and understanding of the parents and the interest on the part of the school people, the prognosis for this boy seems favorable.

Interview with parents of an underachiever

Now let us turn to a case that is somewhat more complicated. Here is a little sixth-grade girl recently entered in the Jackson Elementary School. She came to the attention of the elementary school counselor in this way: The teacher said that the child didn't seem to be interested in her work and that she rarely finished a task. The teacher's question was whether the child was somewhat retarded, though she showed evidences of mental alertness, or whether her seeming lack of self-confidence was keeping her from working to capacity. Would the counselor please test the child, since no test records had been forwarded from the school which she had last attended? This the counselor did and, to the teacher's amazement, found that the child's IQ was 148. What to do now? Certainly they needed to know more about the child, and since they had no information from her former school, the obvious source of help was the parent. A friendly note was sent home and the mother came to school the following week, when the ensuing conference was held:

Mother: *I'm Mrs. Burroughs, Sandra's mother. You wanted to talk to me?*

Counselor: *How do you do, Mrs. Burroughs. I'm Miss Evans, the counselor, and this is Miss Gates, Sandra's teacher. It was good of you to come down this afternoon, Mrs. Burroughs. I'm sure you must be very busy getting established in a new community and all.*

Mother: *Yes, I am busy. But if there's something about Sandra that isn't right—if she isn't getting her work, I certainly can find time to come to school. Is there some difficulty?*

Teacher: *No, Mrs. Burroughs, there isn't any difficulty. It's just that we're very much interested in your little girl, and we feel that if we could know a little more about her, we would be able to be more helpful to her. And, of course, we're always most eager to meet and talk to the parents of all our children, particularly the new ones. We thought perhaps if we knew more about her, her interests and all, we would know better how to challenge her.*

Mother: *Well, I'm not just sure myself what she's interested in. She doesn't seem to want to do much around home. I think she would just sit and play with her dolls, old as she is, if I didn't keep after her. I do insist that she read at least an hour a day. She never has been too good a student; so I feel that I must see to it that she either study or read some good book. Now her older sister Karen has always been an outstanding student. We've been most proud of her. She's a junior in high school and makes straight A's. I wish Sandra could be more like her. Actually, I think she's smart enough, but she just won't work. My husband says I nag at her too much, but she just wouldn't do anything if I didn't make her.*

Counselor: *It's hard to know just how much to push children. It's important that they accomplish things; yet at times pressure doesn't seem to be the answer with them. . . . I didn't know that Sandra had an older sister.*

Mother: *Oh, yes. And if we could just get Sandra to come up to her standards! I'm almost sure that she could if she just would. You tell me she has ability. Some of her other teachers have told me the same thing; yet she never will apply herself. I'm sure I don't know what to do with her. I've taken her privileges away. I've shamed her. I've tried to make her want to be more like Karen. Nothing I do seems to work. She sulks a great deal and goes off by herself.*

Counselor: *Have you noticed any kind of situation in which she responds the way you would like to have her?*

Mother: *Well, when her father pampers her, she seems to be as good as gold for a little while. It doesn't usually last too long. He really spoils her, I think—but you know how fathers are with their daughters!*

Counselor: *Fathers do seem to be partial to their daughters, don't they? What kind of thing does he do that she seems to respond to?*

Mother: *Oh, sometimes she writes a silly little poem— really doesn't amount to anything, and really, from the way he carries on, you'd think she was a second Whittier!*

Counselor: *She responds to his praise?*

Mother: *Does she ever!*

Counselor: *Well, I guess most children do. Praise is important to everybody, but perhaps mostly to children.*

Teacher: *I've noticed that when she gets down to it, she really can produce some nice written work. She seems to have quite original ideas. I haven't given any of the class a chance to write poetry, but Sandra does express herself well in her written work and she seems so pleased when I praise her for it. Praise seems so important to her. I worry a little sometimes because she makes such a good start and then doesn't seem to carry through and finish. I think this bothers me particularly because what she does do is so outstanding. When I've asked her why she didn't finish her work, she has said, "Oh, this is no good." She seems to lack confidence somehow.*

Counselor: *Are we all saying that we have a little girl here who has lots of ability but lacks confidence enough to use all of it? That is true of many people certainly. Maybe Sandra is like that.*

Mother: *I rather doubt that she lacks confidence. It's more likely that she's lazy.*

Teacher: *Well, maybe I haven't challenged her enough. I've been pleased with her written work, particularly when I've let her choose her own topic. Perhaps I should give her more opportunity to be creative and then give her praise and recognition for it if it's good, which it is most likely to be.*

Mother: *But you will see to it that she gets her fundamentals, won't you? This writing I know is good, but I don't want the other things to suffer. . . .*

Teacher: *What would you think if, just for a period of two weeks, we all just use one approach with Sandra—of letting her go along on her own initiative, encouraging her in any of her creative efforts, and giving recognition for a really fine product? Would that be anything that would be worth trying?*

Mother: *I rather doubt it, but nagging her about her school work hasn't seemed to work either. If you think praising her might possibly help, I guess I could try it for two weeks. But I'm not at all sure that I approve of the idea of not making her get all her work done each day.*

Counselor: *I may be all wrong, Mrs. Burroughs, but I have a feeling that Sandra will do more work on her own than we've seen her do since she's been here. I surely can understand your anxiety, however, and you can be sure that we won't go too far on this. And she isn't really likely to get into very bad habits in such a short period. We'll keep in touch with you and let you know how she's getting along in school.*

In this case the mother had a good idea about the child's ability, but to get her to take a positive approach with the youngster was a little difficult. Let's look at the interview.

FIRST Both teacher and counselor were cordial to Sandra's mother and let her know that they were genuinely interested in the child.

SECOND They let the mother know that they thought the child had ability but that they needed her help in knowing better how to challenge the youngster.

THIRD Even though they both probably felt that the mother's method of getting Sandra to do things was not a very good one, they merely accepted it in the beginning and waited for a later and more appropriate time to work in other ideas.

FOURTH The counselor's question, "Have you noticed any kind of situation in which she responds the way you would like to have her?" was a fruitful question because it brought out desirable information which was referred to at a later time.

FIFTH The teacher was quick to pick up the angle of Sandra's having creative ability and took some blame on herself for not having done more about it, quickly indicating what she might do in the immediate future.

SIXTH The teacher did this rather than argue with the mother about Sandra's being lazy.

SEVENTH The counselor gave good information about the challenge and the satisfactions which children with ability get from opportunities to be creative, urging the mother to give Sandra a chance at home. Too, she again stressed the importance of praise for the child.

EIGHTH The teacher picked up the counselor's feeling, at this point, and together they put considerable pressure on the mother. This kind of pressure, as a rule, is not good, but here the attitudes of both teacher and counselor were such that perhaps their tone of voice and their friendly manner assuaged any feelings of resentment that the mother might have had.

NINTH A definite, consistent approach was laid out with both parent and school people accepting their roles and responsibilities; this made it a shared program for Sandra. With the pressure released, she stood a better chance of realizing her potential. The reader might be interested in knowing that in this case the plan proved highly successful.

TENTH It will be noticed that neither counselor nor teacher discussed the social responsibilities of the gifted child with this mother. They were wise not to. This aspect could come in a later conference, after Sandra's underachievement had been given sufficient consideration and attention.

It is gratifying to know that school people have arrived at the point of giving more attention to the gifted child, and it is particularly gratifying to know that they are working together with the parents to do everything possible to help these youngsters realize their potentials. Surely this is one of the finest ways to develop the leadership this country needs.

Conferences
with parents
of mentally retarded
and slow-learning children

CHAPTER TEN

Role of the psychologist Parental attitudes toward their mentally retarded child Interview with parents of a mentally deficient child Interview with parents of a slow-learning child

One of the most deeply disturbing experiences a parent can have is the realization that he has a severely mentally retarded child. In our culture, especially in the middle classes, education is valued as a prerequisite of professional success—a degree of success that cannot be attained by severely retarded children. Parents of such children cannot fail to recognize the handicap early, and they become very much concerned about it, seeking help from pediatrician, school, and other sources. Many parents feel guilty about having such a child. They may be on the defensive about him, or apologetic, or both. They need help in facing the situation realistically and making plans for the child's future, both educational and social.

Role of the psychologist

Ordinarily it is the duty of the psychologist to help parents who face this problem. Diagnosis and recommendations for treatment are the psychologist's, not the teacher's, role. He helps the parents decide whether the child should be placed in a special class or in an institution. This decision depends upon the availability of services, the kind of home, and other factors. If there is no psychologist in the school or school system, the teacher or principal may have to try to interpret the educational opportunities for the child to the parents.

It is important for the psychologist to have established the degree of mental retardation and to know whether it is the primary cause of the child's underachieving. Before any conclusion concerning the placement of the child can be reached, the psychologist should have made a study of the family and should also have obtained the results of individual psychological examinations. Even then any placement should be thought of as being on only a trial basis. Once it seems quite certain that the child is actually mentally retarded, however, the help and cooperation of the parent are essential. As has been stated, this is a most difficult kind of conference because of the very deep feelings of the parents of severely retarded children.

Parental attitudes toward their mentally retarded child

Some parents have many fears about their mentally retarded or mentally deficient child. Will he be able to do anything in school? Will the other children call him dumb or stupid? Will he be easily led astray by brighter children with delinquent tendencies? Will he ever be able to earn a living? What will happen to him when his parents are no longer here to take care of him? Some of these fears are realistic and teachers can help parents face them. Others can be minimized by knowledge. Teachers can explain specifically what a given child can learn and ways in which they help him to learn. They can describe kinds of work he can do—and there are jobs that adolescents with a mental age as low as two or three can perform, though unfortunately there are fewer of these jobs now than in the days before automation. If there are resources in the community for mentally deficient persons, such as the sheltered workshops, parents of the most serious handicapped children should know about them.

Many parents are uncertain as to how to handle a mentally deficient child. In the conference with the psychologist, they can get some information about experiences they can provide at home. If there is a special class for mentally deficient children, the parents can be invited to visit it and see the methods the teacher uses.

Some parents cannot conceal their disappointment or even hatred of their mentally deficient child. It is obviously impossible in parent-teacher conferences to produce a change in such deep-seated attitudes. All the teacher can hope to do is to suggest or, better still, to lead the parents to suggest little ways in which they can change their behavior toward the child. Such changes in behavior are all to the good.

There are parents who are overprotective. They do everything for the mentally deficient child, even to the extent of depriving other children in the family of the opportunities they need. In the conference, the parents may gain some insight into the effect of such overprotection and partiality on the child and on his relations with the other children.

Frequently the teacher has to deal with parents who are on the defensive or who will not admit that their child is mentally deficient. These parents are particularly difficult to interview. Even though they may accept the facts intellectually they cannot accept them emotionally. They expect miracles to happen. The interviewer cannot get anywhere with them. A single interview usually accomplishes little. Only by continued patient work, pointing out the child's positive assets and specific things he can do, can the psychologist make any progress.

The majority of parents of less severely retarded children are uneducated or speak a foreign language and have difficulty in even understanding the problem intellectually. Sometimes a teacher, skillful in communication, can help these parents understand and agree to a modified course of study or placement in a special class or a change in vocational plans. These results were accomplished with Rosie's mother who wanted her child to continue in the academic program, although she was failing and therefore becoming a behavior problem. The teacher was able to get over to the mother these ideas:

"You are worried about Rosie becoming a bad girl."

"Rosie is a good girl, but acting bad because schoolwork is too hard for her."

"Rosie has a job in a restaurant—does job well; feels happy there."

"Rosie does good work with her hands—not so good with her head."

"A home economics course in school would help her to do better the kind of work which she can do well and is happy doing."

"When Rosie is happy, she's a good girl."

"You can help Rosie be a good girl by letting her take the course she can do well."

These ideas finally got through to Rosie's mother, who was genuinely fond of her daughter and wanted her to grow up to be a "good girl."

Sometimes, although the parent tries to be patient, the child's disobedience, destructiveness, and refusal even to try to learn constantly provokes him to wrath. The parent's angry response evokes similar reactions from the child. And so it goes, day after day. With such a situation, the teacher cannot help sympathizing with the parents. Their response to the child is natural. Sometimes, however, parents can be helped to see their role in this vicious cycle and to modify their behavior in the hope that it will in time evoke a more acceptable response on the part of the child.

The interviews in this chapter are with more understanding and better-adjusted parents than those described above. They are more like the interviews a teacher might be expected to help with, although in these cases they were actually held by the psychologist.

One of the first ways of relieving the parent's feelings is the discussion of objective data about the child—to help the parent both to express the ways he has observed the child to be relatively slow in growing and to realize that such causes as illness, birth injury, or accident may have been responsible for the child's condition. This seems to relieve the parent somewhat of a feeling of personal responsibility for the child's handicap and helps to develop the concept of a slowly developing child rather than that of a permanently retarded child.

Interview with parents of a mentally deficient child

Let us turn now to a reported interview between the psychologist who has been working with eight-year-old Linda, whose IQ he has determined to be about 48, and Linda's mother, an intelligent woman who also has a bright older boy. The mother, a college graduate, has found it very difficult to accept the fact that the little girl is so slow.

Mother: *I got your letter. I understand you have been testing my little girl Linda and that you want to talk to me.*

Psychologist: *Yes, we've been making a study of your child. She's a lovable little girl, isn't she?*

Mother: *Oh, do you think so? We do, but we've worried because she is so slow.*

Psychologist: *We're very much interested in your child, Mrs. Richards, and we want to help you make the best possible educa-*

tional plans for her. We need to know more about Linda, her development, her background, her interests, etc. You know more about your child than anyone else and can give us a great deal of help. Would you tell me a little more about her developmental background? For instance, was she a full-term baby—and was there anything unusual about the birth?

Mother: *She was a full-term baby and birth seemed quite normal, although the doctor had a hard time making her start to breathe.*

Psychologist: *And at what ages did she walk and talk?*

Mother: *She walked at the usual age, but she was quite slow in talking. She was over four, actually.*

Psychologist: *Has she ever had any serious illnesses or accidents?*

Mother: *Well, she had a bad bump on her head about a year ago, but after the X rays were taken, the doctor felt there was no brain damage.*

Psychologist: *Would you tell me a little about your family?*

Mother: *Linda has a brother, who is twelve. He's real smart and makes very good grades in school. He seems a lot like me. . . . Linda's daddy seemed a little slow in developing, but he did manage to graduate from college, too. Linda is so like him, in a way. Do you think maybe she might suddenly begin to develop and—and—maybe be able to go to college? What did your tests show?*

Psychologist: *Well, at present, she seems to be functioning more like a five-year-old than an eight-year-old. When she is ten, she will probably be functioning more like a seven-year-old. You know that every child develops at his own rate—some faster, some slower than average. Linda seems to be a child who, for some reason, has been slowed up in development. You have noticed the difference between the development of Linda and that of your son?*

Mother: *Oh, yes! As I said, he gets along so well at school, gets his homework in, and gets A's in almost everything. He walked and talked much earlier than Linda did, and he's always been a child who likes to play with other children. Linda is very shy, you know, and just hates school. Oh, I just didn't think I would ever have a retarded child!* (Cries.)

Psychologist: *The important thing, Mrs. Richards, is, if possible, not to think of her as a retarded child, but how we can best develop the capabilities she has. Have you thought of what abilities she does possess?*

Mother: *Well, she is pretty, don't you think?*

Psychologist: *Yes indeed, she is an unusually pretty child. She also seems to have learned little ways of getting along with people.*

Mother: *She really gets along quite well with older people, but she's shy with the youngsters of her own age. She likes most to be with me and to help me in the house.*

Psychologist: *She apparently feels most secure when she is with you, and it is important that she have lots of reassurance and affection. What things does she do that you can be proud of?*

Mother: *She likes to help me with the dishes and house-work, and she likes to make cookies. Of course, I have to help her with the recipe. She seems quite normal at home. That's why it's so hard to understand why she doesn't seem to be able to learn like the other children in school, and she's so unhappy there.*

Psychologist: *That's one thing I wanted to talk to you about, Mrs. Richards. We want to try to prevent her from developing feelings of inferiority in school or in regard to school-work. There are many other children who are very much like Linda and who have these same feelings. For this reason, our school system has provided special classes that are more suited to their needs and capacities.*

Mother: *Who are the children who go there? Aren't they quite different from Linda?*

Psychologist: *They are all youngsters who are slower in*

learning ability. They are usually much happier in this situation because they can hold their own with other children for the first time in their school lives.

Mother: *Do they learn things there like reading and arithmetic and everything?*

Psychologist: *Yes, very definitely! It's just that the specially trained teachers take these children at a slower rate in these subjects and in much smaller groups so that each one can proceed at his own pace. They also learn to do cooking, sewing, and other useful things.*

Mother: *Linda would like that.*

Psychologist: *I'm sure she would. But perhaps you would like to visit one of these classes before we place Linda in one. Would you?*

Mother: *Oh yes, I would! When could I go?*

Psychologist: *How about next Monday morning, say at ten o'clock?*

Mother: *That would be fine. If the school makes special provision for children like Linda, I guess we ought to take advantage of it.*

Psychologist: *Perhaps after you have visited the class, you would like to talk with me again about ways of making it seem a privilege to Linda and preparing the family to cooperate in this way.*

Mother: *Oh, I would appreciate help in that. I've been wondering what to say to her.*

Psychologist: *We will help you with that. Good-bye, now.*

Mother: *Good-bye.*

This was not an easy interview, but it was very well handled, wasn't it? Let us review the steps that the psychologist took and see what actually happened.

FIRST   He complimented the child to the mother—probably a rare thing for this mother. It perhaps helped to give the mother a feeling that here was someone who would be acceptant of her child.

SECOND   He let the mother know how interested he was in the child and enlisted the mother's aid, giving her a feeling of importance. The mother was made to feel that *she* was the one who really knew this child and who could help the psychologist in studying her.

THIRD   In drawing the mother out about the child's family, the psychologist helped her to see the difference in the rate of development between her normal son and this child. Following this, he merely indicated that every child developed at a different rate; this was initially easy for the parent to accept. Later, the mother may be able to accept the fact that the child can never reach a normal adult level of intelligence.

FOURTH   The psychologist led the mother into concentrating on what the child *could* do rather than on her shortcomings. It helped the mother to feel that there were things the child could do and that here was someone who recognized those things as being important.

FIFTH   In regard to the school problem, the psychologist let the mother know that there were many children who were like Linda and who were ever so much happier in the special-class situation, where they could all go along at their own pace.

SIXTH   He was able to reassure the mother that the child would learn to do many of the fundamental processes under conditions that would be far more comfortable for her.

SEVENTH   To make sure that the mother would be satisfied with the special class, he invited her to visit it, thus assuring her that she was not being sold a bill of goods. This was wise even though the mother might be disturbed by the appearance and manners of some of the children in the class. The psychologist promised to help her with this phase of the placement.

Perhaps the most important thing throughout this whole interview was the kindly, sympathetic attitude of the psychologist.

It is interesting to note that many parents of mentally retarded children become overprotective and actually spend more time and energy with him than they would a normal child, often to the detriment of other children in the family.

Unfortunately, some parents are led to believe that such a child will grow out of it; this is indeed most unlikely, and to suggest it certainly is unfair to the parents. If the child is definitely mentally retarded, it is far kinder to help the parents gradually face the situation realistically and make suitable plans than to bolster their hopes and keep the poor child in an unfortunate position of having to compete with others far beyond him mentally. The important thing is to help the parent concentrate on what the child can do and on how to develop to the fullest his potential for becoming a useful member of society.

Parents of seriously mentally retarded children often go through four stages of thinking and feeling as they talk with an understanding person in a series of interviews:

1. They mourn the loss of the child they expected to have. They ask, "Why did this happen to me? Is it because of something I have done or failed to do?"
2. They resent the person who tells them the truth about their child and go to someone else for reassurance.
3. They come back eventually to the person who has been honest with them.
4. They gradually come around to accepting the situation: "I don't like what happened, but I'll see what I can do for my mentally retarded child and for the other children in my family, for whom having a mentally retarded brother or sister is a heavy burden." Having arrived at this attitude, they are often helpful to other parents.

The interviewer does not tell them what to do; he does not pressure them. If it seems best to put the child in an institution, he will describe the advantages and disadvantages of institutions. As there is usually a long waiting list for such placement, the interviewer may suggest that the parents put their child's name on it even if they are undecided. Then if anything happens to the parents or if they change their attitude about institutions, the child will be provided for.

With parents who themselves are mentally retarded, the interviewer would have to use a different approach. He would have to tell them specifically what to do, but try to make them feel that they are making the decision.

Interview with parents of a slow-learning child

A similar kind of interview that school people find difficult to handle is the one with the parent of a child who is normal in many ways but who, unfortunately, has somewhat limited mental capacity. In many cases these parents are of low socioeconomic status; they do not realize their child's limitations and may be unaware that he is below the average in mental ability; they are not much concerned about his school progress. They are the parents who do not attend the school meetings or seek help for the child.

Occasionally there are parents of higher socioeconomic levels who early see the difference between the retarded child and other children in their family or among their friends' children. These parents tend to put too much pressure on the child or too much pressure on the teacher. It is very difficult for the teacher to help the parent face the situation realistically. As has been said before, the parent's ego is so involved with the success of his child that being realistic in regard to his child's limited intelligence is hard for him.

The following interview was a difficult one for the teacher.

Mrs. Huston reports that Dick, a sixth-grade boy, thirteen years old, was finding the sixth-grade work frustrating. The boy had spent two years in the fifth grade and was promoted to the sixth only because of age and social adjustment. His IQ on the Binet, given at age ten, was recorded as 80. Dick's mother had been told earlier, according to a notation in his folder, that the boy seemed to find schoolwork very difficult. The mother had said that her older boy had been a slow starter, too, but had grown out of it; she was sure Dick would do the same thing. Feeling that the mother needed to be aware of the situation before Dick got into junior high school, Mrs. Huston decided to invite her to school for a conference. She knew it wouldn't be easy, and she wasn't sure how she would handle it.

A cordial note home brought the mother to school the following week, when she and the teacher had the following talk. Mrs. Huston recorded as much of it as was possible.

Teacher: *How do you do. I'm Mrs. Huston, Dick's teacher. I'm so glad you could find time to come down to see me.*

Mother: *I'm glad to meet you, too. Dick has spoken about you often. Dick's a good boy. He always seems to like his teachers.*

Teacher: *Dick is a good boy. He helps me do many things in the room here. I've been interested in him from the very first of the year. He likes to keep our blackboards clean and helps me put away some of our materials almost every night. I imagine he helps you a lot at home, too, doesn't he?*

Mother: *Yes, he's pretty good help—especially with the baby. He just adores her. Loves to take her out in her buggy. I can't let him take her too far away. Sometimes he gets interested in something else and forgets her. You know how boys are. But I don't know how I'd get along without his help with her. How do you think he's getting along in school this year? He's doing better, don't you think? He was rather a slow starter—his brother was, too. They kept Dick back in the fifth grade, you know. I thought it was a mistake, but I thought the school people ought to know what they were doing. Course he can't spell very well yet; but most kids can't these days. He's reading better this year, but it seems he ought to do better than he does. What do you think?*

Teacher: *Well, Dick does seem to find spelling and read-*
ing pretty hard. Some youngsters always do. Dick may be one
of them. He has improved this year, but the going does seem
pretty rough for him. That was one reason I wanted to talk
to you.

Mother: *Now, you're not going to tell me you want to hold*
him back another year, are you? Because I just wouldn't allow
it again.

Teacher: *Oh, no. I don't think that will be necessary. But*
since he does seem to be having a hard time, I thought that
maybe you and I ought to talk about it a little and see what we
could both do to help him.

Mother: *Well, I didn't want him held back again because*
I know he's going to pick up. You said he'd improved a lot this
year. Don't you think maybe he's found himself now and will
do all right now?

Teacher: *Well, now he has improved, but perhaps not*
what we would call "a lot." You said that you felt Dick didn't
read as well as he should. Actually, he is reading at what we'd
say was a high third-grade level, and he's in the low sixth. Now,
I'm hoping that with some extra help, he will reach the fourth-
grade level by the end of the year.

Mother: *Oh, my goodness, is it that bad? Why haven't his*
teachers taught him better? I just don't know that I go for these
modern teaching methods. Seems to me we learned to read a
lot earlier than Dick. My other boy had some trouble, too.

Teacher: *School may always be hard for Dick, Mrs. Paulsen,*
but fortunately he has such a good disposition and is so friendly
and polite with people that he'll make out all right. It's true
that he is retarded in his schoolwork, but there are lots of people
in this world who never learn to read beyond the fourth-grade
level, and they are able to make a good living and be good citi-
zens. Dick can probably progress beyond that, if we help him,
and there will be ever so many things that he will be able to do.
You've helped him so much to get along with people. If peo-

ple like him and he continues to do really well the things that he can do and likes to do, he'll get along just fine.

Mother: You're telling me my boy isn't very bright, aren't you? How do you know he isn't? I think that he just hasn't had good teachers.

Teacher: I didn't say just that, Mrs. Paulsen, but rather that perhaps the things that he can do best may not be in the academic field. Everyone who does the socially useful work he can do best is needed. We shall try to give Dick enough academic learning to get along in this world. We need to plan a program in which he will be successful. I know that's what you want for him.

Mother: Of course I do, but we had thought we'd send him to the junior college here and then see whether he should go on to the university or to some trade school. We hadn't thought much beyond that. Don't you think he could go on to junior college?

Teacher: Time will tell. I don't think we can say for certain now, Mrs. Paulsen. But I am going to be frank with you, as I know you want me to be, and tell you that it is my honest opinion that Dick may not be able to take the academic course in a junior college. However, in some of the junior colleges, short-term training courses are being offered which equip students to enter semiskilled trades. I can't tell you much about them, but it might be something that you would want to look into later on. The thing that we're both interested in, I'm sure, is to help Dick succeed in his present schoolwork. Isn't that right?

Mother: Yes, of course. And I still think that he'll pick up in his studies.

Teacher: That's just why I asked you to come down today, Mrs. Paulsen, to see if together we can't help Dick to pick up. Your encouragement of him in any way would be helpful—his homework or books I give him to read in school. I'll give him as much individual attention as I can. I worry a little about his going into junior high school, and we want to do everything *possible to get him ready. They do have some groups there that move a little more slowly than others. I think that Dick will get along pretty well in one of those if we help him all we can now.*

Mother: *Now, what are these groups that move slowly? Are they dumbbell kids? I don't want him in with them.*

Teacher: *They are called opportunity classes and are made up of youngsters who find academic work more difficult than some of the others do; so the schools have set up classes that are a little smaller and which move just a little bit more slowly. The youngsters get more individual attention in these classes and are able to learn more than they could in a bigger class where the pace is so much faster. I'm sure Dick would get along well in such a group. . . . Thank you ever so much for coming and please come whenever you feel that you'd like to discuss Dick and his work.*

The teacher could not give the mother definite answers to all her questions. That was the role of the psychologist, rather than the teacher. But let's see now what she did.

FIRST   A cordial note home and a cordial greeting established an initially friendly relationship.

SECOND   She told the mother that Dick was a good boy and had been very helpful.

THIRD   Every time the mother seemed at all critical of the school people, the teacher remained silent, never getting on the defensive.

FOURTH   She made it clear that Dick needed help and that the mother and she had a shared responsibility in encouraging him in his schoolwork.

FIFTH   She was honest in her evaluation of Dick's work, telling the mother exactly where he stood in relation to his grade level.

SIXTH   All the while that she was talking of Dick's academic limitations, she kept emphasizing Dick's good qualities and what he *would* be able to do. She accentuated the positive throughout. She also made it clear that Dick was just one of many who find academic work difficult.

SEVENTH   She gave the mother an honest opinion regarding college possibilities, based on the psychologist's report, stating that he *probably* could not make the academic course, but that she understood there were other possibilities. She did not pretend to have all the answers regarding the college courses, but merely suggested that the parents look into what was offered. She was not foolish enough to make any absolute statements, knowing full well that many educators have made grave mistakes in estimating a child's potentialities.

EIGHTH   She helped the mother to think positively in regard to Dick's future happiness and usefulness.

NINTH   She further expressed interest and concern about the boy's adjustment to the junior high school situation. She felt that the mother should be prepared for the possibility that Dick would be placed in the slow-moving group in the junior high school, assuring her that this would be a good placement for him.

TENTH   She enlisted the mother's aid in giving the boy an extra boost by working with him at night. This would have a twofold result: the extra drill would help the boy somewhat, and the special attention and manifested interest from his mother would be encouraging to him.

ELEVENTH   One imporant thing which she neglected to do was to suggest to the mother the importance of providing experiences for this boy in which he would feel successful.

Teachers and parents together can help the slow-learning child by working and planning together for his welfare. If the facts are faced realistically, then constructive plans can be based on what the child *can* do, not on what he can't do.

Vocational counseling with parent and child

CHAPTER ELEVEN

Building right attitudes toward work   Guidance in the elementary school   Guidance in the high school   An exploratory interview with a high-average student   Interviews with below-average students

How many thousands of high school seniors come up to graduation time still uncertain about their position in the world of work! In this fast-moving age of science, changes are taking place so rapidly that one can hardly focus on a given occupation before its qualifications are modified and its demand for workers increases or decreases. The student may be *perplexed* by this vocational panorama, but parents are downright *worried*.

Parents are so involved emotionally with their child that it is difficult and sometimes almost impossible for them to be realistic in their evaluation of their child's potential. Most often they tend to feel that the child is brighter than he actually is and that college preparation for a profession is the only future for him. Other parents, for one reason or another, underestimate the capacity of their child. Many, of course, are able to evaluate their offspring quite realistically.

Both parents and the child need to gain insights which will enable them to come to some sensible conclusions as to the general field or fields of occupations for which the youngster might have the most to offer. Counselors and teachers can be of great help to them by bringing together and interpreting to them results of intelligence tests, achievement tests, occupational-aptitude tests, interest inventories, grades, and other objective materials.

Building right attitudes toward work

Although self-understanding is very important in the process of making a vocational choice, gaining a positive feeling toward the dignity of work itself, whatever it may entail, is also important. The garbage man has long been disparaged, as has the charwoman. They have been thought of as low on the ladder of success. Yet probably these two groups of people have contributed as much to the health of the country as some of the professional groups. They are doing positive, preventive work. But how do we help our students and parents to realize that these people and thousands of other people in jobs other than the professions contribute greatly to the welfare of the country and that every job has dignity if it is socially useful?

Perhaps the best way to build attitudes toward the world of work is to begin with youngsters in the elementary grades. We have observed an occupational unit in grades as low as the second. Here youngsters have set up "play" stores, post offices, gas stations, railroad stations, piers, and other places of business. A ship's captain brings his ship (made by him) up to the pier, stevedores unload his cargo, truck drivers arrive with trucks (made by them) and load the cargo. The trucks proceed to the railroad station or directly to the store. In the latter case, the storekeeper receives the cargo and sets it up for business, so that it is ready for the consumer. Obviously, trucks are sometimes low on gas, and so the station attendant has to "fill 'er up." And some days, when class members have written letters, the post office business booms. In all cases, ships, trucks, stores, post offices, all have to be swept out and cleaned for tomorrow.

Good teachers make the most of teaching youngsters about what each worker's job is in this occupationally oriented dramatic-play unit. Naturally, as the youngsters progress into upper grades, the units on occupations become more encompassing and youngsters are encouraged to read and to make reports on various fields of work.

Guidance in the elementary school

As has been indicated in an earlier chapter, it is most important for teachers to begin to help parents to realize the approximate potential of their child while the child is still in the elementary grades. Caution should always be taken against making unconditional predictions or statements. Rather, statements should be factual, as "Tommy may find academic work very difficult all through school," or "Nancy is doing her work as we would expect an average third grader should," or "Jim works very quickly and with fine comprehension. We can expect him to be an excellent student if we can continue to stimulate his interest."

Any time the elementary teacher has the opportunity for a parent conference in which he would be likely to make any of the above statements, he also has the opportunity to point out the vast number and variety of careers open to youth at all ability levels. As the child moves along, his interests and abilities should be observed so that ultimately he will enter an appropriate vocation which will contribute to the welfare of the nation and consequently give him a great deal of satisfaction. This may all seem quite idealistic, but it is realistic in that it will help parents to begin to think about their child's future with reference to a wide variety of vocations, not just the professional and white-collar jobs.

If the elementary teachers, counselors, and/or administrators can stimulate this kind of thinking on the part of the parents and the youngsters themselves, then the high school teachers and counselors can build on that foundation and help the student to choose a career commensurate with his potential and interests.

In the elementary school, the teacher who is in direct contact with the child for most of the school day assumes the major responsibility for the guidance of the child and his parents. Elementary school counselors work with and through teachers. They may demonstrate classroom techniques of child study, conduct a workshop on parent-teacher conferences, and supply books, pamphlets, pictures, films, and charts about vocations suitable at different grade levels. Since the amount of time counselors can spend in each school is limited, they will have interviews or play therapy sessions only with students presenting the more complex problems. They will have conferences and special small discussion groups only with the parents with whom teachers find it most difficult to work. As part of their job, the elementary school counselors will also supply test results needed by the teacher and hold meetings with groups of teachers. The counselor will also participate in any PTA meetings related to the subject of guidance.

Guidance in the high school

Adolescence presents special problems. As children grow up, most parents have fewer contacts with the schools; systematic parent-teacher conferences have too often been discontinued. The parent often feels unable to help. Yet there is much that parents can do to give the youngster stability in these transitional years between childhood and adulthood.

Adolescence is often a period of anxiety for both parents and adolescents. Parents feel at a loss. They do not know how to help a child with his high school work. One boy said, "Parents pay a lot of attention to their preschool and elementary school children, but neglect them when they grow older. My mother is never home after school. She doesn't know where I am. For all she knows, I might be ten miles away robbing a bank." A gifted adolescent girl wrote, "There is nothing more comforting to a worried and confused adolescent than parents whom they feel they can go to freely and get aid on a problem good or bad—aid from parents who will understand. Truly the children I feel genuine pity for . . . are those who don't feel that they can confide in their parents." [1] This is a good description of the parents' role during their children's adolescent years: to maintain a supporting relationship but not to dominate; to assist but not insist—except on a few firmly held limits; and to emphasize the positive in the adolescent's more or less unstable behavior.

In the high school, various persons will take responsibility for educational and vocational guidance, depending upon the kind of guidance program. The full-time counselor can be expected to have the most comprehensive and technical information about the individual student and about educational and vocational opportunities. In small schools or in large schools with a staff of full-time counselors, the specially trained counselor may do most of the vocational counseling of parents and students.

In other schools organized into small guidance units, such as the homeroom or teacher-counselor program, teacher-counselors conduct most of the interviews with parents and students. The role of the full-time counselor is to provide the teacher-counselors with continuous in-service education and with the occupational and educational guidance information they need. The counselor also serves as a resource for the referral of baffling and time-consuming cases.

In a school having neither a full-time nor a part-time counselor, members of the faculty with special interests may be delegated to help parents and their children make appropriate educational and vocational plans. For example, a teacher with three children who would soon be ready to enter college assumed responsibility for the college guidance, while another teacher,

[1] Ruth Strang, *The Adolescent Views Himself*, New York, McGraw-Hill Book Company, Inc., 1957. pp. 95, 170.

who was well acquainted with the world of work through personal experience and wide reading, held most of the conferences with parents and students concerning choice of vocation.

Subject teachers, knowing a certain student very well, may also talk with parents about the child's tentative educational and vocational plans and refer those who need more expert help or technical information to other persons. When asked questions about educational and vocational opportunities which they cannot answer accurately, teachers should never hesitate to say, "I don't know," and then refer the parent or student to some source of accurate, up-to-date information.

Although the interviews reported in this chapter were actually held by a trained counselor, a teacher-counselor could learn to conduct this kind of conference quite skillfully.

One of the best ways for teachers to learn the necessary skills is to observe a more highly trained counselor in action. Next best is to read recorded verbatim interviews.

An exploratory interview with a high-average student

Let us assume that some foundation has been laid by elementary school personnel in the field of vocations and that Gary Phillips has progressed to the ninth grade. He is a high-average student with a composite IQ of 109. He is not entirely sure of what he wishes to do when he finishes school. His parents would like him to take work beyond high school, but it is not likely that there will be much money available for this. At the present time, Gary is enrolled in a social studies course in which students are introduced to the world of work through a study of different occupations and careers.

The ninth-grade counselor works very closely with the social studies teacher in his unit, routing "live" vocational materials to her, talking to the group, and helping her to locate inspirational speakers who can interest the youngsters in examining the world of work and make them think about what every working person, through a socially useful job, contributes to society. The counselor can help teachers develop in students a constructive and realistic attitude toward the various fields of occupation and, in general, fire up the interest in Gary and other youngsters to study seriously their own abilities and interests in relation to possible opportunities of the future.

The ninth-grade counselor feels that this is an appropriate time to bring Gary's parents into the picture and to help Gary and his parents think about vocations in a broad way. She has worked out her own schedule so that she will be able to have a conference with the parents of all ninth graders. She has gathered together and recorded on each ninth grader's cumulative record his grades, his mental-ability-test scores, his achievement-test scores, his interest profile, his vocational-aptitude-test profile, and other pertinent data.

The counselor is ready now to contact Gary's parents and invite them to a conference. The following is the letter she sends home.

Jefferson Junior High School
December, 1963

The Ninth-grade Social Studies course of study includes a unit called "The Personal, Social, and Vocational Problems of Youth." It is designed to help the student understand himself and others; to plan a study program for high school; and to make tentative plans for a career.

This year there is increased emphasis on the career-guidance phase of the unit. Our efforts have been directed toward helping each student make a reasonably objective appraisal of his own abilities, weaknesses, interests, ambitions, etc. Each student is required to make a serious study of "The World of Work," particularly in the areas of his own vocational interests. This appraisal and study should result in a more realistic objective for your child's career.

In addition to the regular guidance program, the ninth-grade students have been given a series of aptitude and interest tests. The test results plus the student's scholastic-achievement record will be used in a half-hour Evaluation and Planning Conference with your child and you. Long-range career plans will be discussed and a tentative high school program will be considered.

The conferences are being scheduled for January, February, March, and April. For the convenience of those parents who cannot come during the day, an evening conference will be scheduled. Each individual conference will last approximately thirty minutes. You will receive a note from this office (via your child) confirming the conference date and time, if you will kindly indicate your preference on the form below. The school needs and welcomes the help and cooperation of the parents in this program.

Sincerely,

Jean Moore

Ninth-grade Counselor
Geneva 8–5701

(Please detach and return to school.)

Ninth-grade Career Guidance Evaluation and Planning Conference

Student's Name   Social Studies Teacher   Period
(Last name first)

Parent's Name   Home Phone

Please schedule me for a conference in January _____
February _____
March   _____
April   _____

I would prefer a morning _____ (9:45–12:00)
afternoon _____ (1:15– 5:00)
evening   _____ (6:15– 9:15)

Comments: _____

_____

_____

_____
Parent's Signature

After the counselor has invited the parents and has received a reply from them indicating their preference for an approximate date and time, she will send the following note of confirmation home via the student.

Jefferson Junior High School
Ninth-grade Career Guidance
Evaluation and Planning Conference

_____
(Please deliver to your parents)

_____
Date issued

_____
Social Studies Class

Dear Parents:

We are pleased to confirm your appointment for the Ninth-grade Career Guidance Conference for

_____
Month   Date   Time

If you cannot attend at the above time, please call or write on the back of this sheet and return it to me.

You are welcome to spend some time in the school library, before or after the conference, studying the vocational guidance materials.

When possible, we should prefer to have the student and parents come together so that we may share all our ideas and hopefully come to some tentative conclusions toward long-term planning for appropriate vocational goals for your child.

Sincerely,

Jean Moore

Ninth-grade Counselor
Geneva 8–5701

The above letters have gone out to the parents of all ninth-grade students; so naturally Gary's father and mother, Mr. and Mrs. Phillips, have received them and have an appointment with Miss Moore. Here is a summary of the significant points in their conference.

Miss Moore: *Hello. I'm Miss Moore. Won't you come in? Hi, Gary, how are you? I'm glad all three of you could come in today. I hope it wasn't too hard for you to get away.*

Mr. Phillips: *Well, it wasn't too hard, and anyway we thought this sounded like a pretty important conference. We don't know what Gary ought to be, and I don't think he has any idea either. Time he was thinking about it, though.*

Miss Moore: *Most students haven't—and probably shouldn't have—settled on a particular occupation at this time, Mr. Phillips. But we think that some exploration of the various vocational fields is in order now, and we feel that with the help of you and Mrs. Phillips and a study of Gary's record and test scores, Gary may decide in what general field or fields he may want to study as a possible future vocation. He may change his mind several times along the way, but it's time for him to begin to think about his future.*

Mrs. Phillips: *I agree with you. I even know of several college students who have no idea as to what they want to do.*

Miss Moore: *Gary, when I talked to you last, you said you didn't know whether you could or should go on to college. Have you talked about this recently with your parents?*

Gary: *We've talked some, but we haven't decided. If I do go, I'll be going to a junior college and working some on the side. We have a good-sized family, you know.*

Miss Moore: *Yes, I do know. But isn't it fine that we have such a good junior college here if it seems best for you to continue on past high school?*

Gary: *It sure is.*

Miss Moore: *Well, let's take a look at your total record here.* (To parents.) *Gary has a good capacity to learn, and he has worked hard. He has almost a B average, as you know. Gary, did you tell your folks about those long tests you took in English and arithmetic when you came into junior high?*

Gary: *Yes, I think I did.*

Mrs. Phillips: *Yes, he did. He said that you told him that he was above average in math, but just about average in English. How good is that?*

Miss Moore: *He actually scored at the 66th percentile on his math test, which means that he did as well as, or better than, 66 per cent of all the students in the country who took this test. You see, this is a test used in school districts all over the country; so when I say he did as well as, or better than, 66 per cent of the students who took this test, that means students from all over the country. Now, on his English test, his score was in the 44th percentile—still within average range. He did as well as, or better than, 44 per cent of the students throughout the country who took this test. He seems to be a little stronger in math than English. His grades indicate this too. Gary, is it that you like math better than English?*

Gary: *Yes, I do like it better, but maybe it's because it's a little easier for me. . . .*

Mrs. Phillips: *I've tried to help him with his English, but I'm pretty rusty myself; so "we" haven't done so well, have we, Gary?*

Miss Moore: *Gary, as I look at your profile on your interest test, I find that you scored highest in the clerical and persuasive areas. Have you ever been interested in trying to sell anything?*

Gary:*Well, I work as a box boy on Saturdays at Johnny's grocery store, and once in a while I get to help the customers find things. Sometimes I talk them into something better than they're looking for. It's kind of fun. You can't make a living doing that, though.*

Miss Moore: *You know there are lots of things to sell besides groceries and many ways of selling besides following people around in a business establishment.*

Mr. Phillips: *Well, I don't know how good he is at selling things, but I can tell you he sure gets around us by selling ideas —for some reason we have twin pipes and two carburetors on our car! The car seemed to run just fine the way it was, but Gary got it into his head that we'd be far better off if we added a pipe and a carburetor. I had no intention of doing this but—well, we have them now.*

Miss Moore: *Well, Gary, it sounds as though you have indicated a small interest and some practical demonstrations in the ability to sell. Let's see if your aptitude-test scores bear this out. Here they are. Yes, as a matter of fact, they do to some extent. At any rate they don't rule out your abilities in this line. I wonder whether we haven't come upon something for you to explore further. You know selling things is just a small part of a very large field of occupations called merchandising.*

Mr. Phillips: *That's right. I visited a friend once who was the manager of a department store; he took me all through the various departments and showed me all the different ways they used to get their customers to buy things. And he told me about his buyers, what they did; his advertising specialists and what they did; his display specialists and all kinds of things. I had no idea there was so much to it. Very interesting. How do you get into that kind of thing? Do you have to start as a clerk?*

Miss Moore: *Not necessarily. Gary mentioned that if he went to college, he would undoubtedly go to our junior college here. Well, the technical division of the college carries the regular academic course of study, but in addition they have a course in merchandising that offers study in many different kinds of mer-*

chandising and, as a matter of fact, actual experience in various activity-type classes. He could combine the two. Does this have any appeal for you at all, Gary?

Gary: *As much as anything, I guess. We're studying vocations in our social studies class now. I guess I could study about merchandising as well as anything else.*

Mrs. Phillips: *What kind of course would he have to take in high school to go into that?*

Miss Moore: *He would do well to combine an academic course with some business courses. We could work this out very nicely. He would take his regular academic courses in English, science, math, history, and all the other requirements for college entrance. In addition, we should want to be sure that he worked in typing, two years of bookkeeping, computing machines, and possibly a course or two in art and public speaking. I should like him to talk to the head of our commercial department before we lay out his final three-year program. He would get his real training in the merchandising course at the junior college or on the job. But the courses I have mentioned would help him to explore this general field as well as to lay a good foundation for his future studies.*

Mr. Phillips: *You know, this sounds as if it has possibilities. What do you think, Son?*

Gary: *It's O.K. Good as any. Can I change my mind if I don't like it after I study it?*

Miss Moore: *Sure, Gary. This is only one suggestion to begin with. There are many fields that you can explore as you go along, and you should learn to explore and study other fields. It seems as though this were a natural one just to start with. . . . Regular college work may be a little difficult for you. You can probably do it if you study hard. But vocational success, studies have shown, depends a lot on getting along with people on the job. You are outgoing and like people and seem to have persuasive ability.*

Gary: *Hope you're right.*

Miss Moore (to parents): *You two have a fine boy here.*

He stands a good chance of doing well in the vocation he eventually settles on in line with his abilities and interests. We are interested in helping him to evaluate his strengths and weaknesses with reference to both his educational and his vocational goals. He'll learn more about himself as he goes along, and he'll learn more about the various occupations too. Your boy has good average ability; he is a hard worker; and the other students like him. That's a good combination.

Mr. Phillips: *Thank you very much, Miss Moore. You know, this gives us something to think about. We were a bit worried because we didn't really know too much about what Gary could or couldn't do. He isn't one to say too much what he's interested in, either.*

Mrs. Phillips: *That's right, but this conference has been most helpful.*

Miss Moore: *It's been pleasant for me too. . . . Gary, you are welcome to come in here any time; and if you decide, after doing your study on merchandising, that this isn't the field for you, come in and we'll explore something else. You see, we're just getting started. . . . Good-bye, and do come again.*

Let us review now the steps the counselor took to get Gary into a thoughtful state of mind regarding his future.

FIRST   She has worked very closely with Gary's social studies teacher in the occupations unit, helping the teacher to find information and to use materials she has provided. She has talked to the classes and helped the teacher to secure inspirational and well-informed speakers who could stimulate the youngsters to enter enthusiastically into the study of a field of occupations.

SECOND   She set up a schedule of conferences so that she could interview Gary's parents and the parents of all his classmates.

THIRD   She sent a cordial note home offering a wide range of choices for an appointment for an individual conference with both parents and Gary, so that all four could sit together and evaluate his achievements and potentialities.

FOURTH When the parents and Gary arrived, she had at her finger tips all of Gary's test scores and other important data which would be of help in making some tentative plans for his future.

FIFTH She was friendly and warm as she interpreted the scores; yet she was quite honest in pointing up the fact that Gary might have a bit of a struggle to succeed in college on the basis of his test scores and high school grades.

SIXTH Pulling together the scores of the aptitude and the interest tests, Gary's selling experience in the store and his stated interest in it, his general ability, and his personality trait of "outgoingness," she suggested the vast field of merchandising.

SEVENTH She indicated that the local junior college had a fine course in this field; here he could receive his training and also take further academic work if he desired.

EIGHTH While she pointed out that this might be the field which would interest him most, she also made it very clear that the experience should be exploratory and the goal tentative. He was free to change his mind at any time.

NINTH She gave the parents the assurance that they had a fine son who would get along well and that the school personnel would watch his progress with real interest.

TENTH She left the door open for Gary and/or the parents to come back whenever any one of them wished to.

This seems to have been a relatively simple conference because Gary was a high-average, hard-working student, with co-operative parents. Actually, it *was* relatively simple, but yet very important. The series of events from the beginning of the occupational unit in the social studies class to the conference with his parents and counselor, at which a tentative plan was made, and then to the actual study of the field of merchandising served to put Gary into a thoughtful mood regarding his future. He may never go into the field of merchandising, but he has begun to get some insight into his own strengths, weaknesses, and potentialities. He has begun to think of himself with reference to the future. He is now really beginning to realize the importance of thinking about a vocational goal. He is learning how to make a study of an occupation: what it entails, the qualifications, personal and academic, the type of work, the hours, the salary, and many other important facts relevant to any occupation.

We have said that this was an important conference for Gary. It would be equally important for any other student who is approximately his age or older. All youngsters need help in getting the most objective view of themselves as a basis for setting up realistic vocational goals.

Interviews with below-average students

Counselors often say, "It's not too difficult to have parent conferences together with the child when the child is relatively bright, but how do you handle them when the child has an IQ between 75 and 90?" Obviously, this is a more difficult conference to manage, particularly if the parents cannot accept the fact that the youngster is not at least an average student.

The elementary school personnel must take a large share of the responsibility in preparing the parents along the way to be realistic about their child's relative potentiality. When objective data have been gathered by the teacher and/or counselor or administrator about a given child, these data need to be interpreted honestly to the parent. IQ scores should never be given out for reasons stated before, but the achievement-test scores, class performance, and the relative potential of the child can and should be discussed and interpreted. If this is done in a kindly way, as suggested earlier in this chapter, then neither child nor parents will be shocked when the child receives his first secondary school report card, on which grades are recorded according to his rating among other students in the class. Also, parents will be better prepared to make realistic plans for the future when the child reaches the age for beginning to focus on a vocational goal.

Let us assume that Jack has reached the ninth grade and that very little evidence has been given the parents by the elementary school personnel that he is not at least an average student. The parents have been concerned during his first two years in junior high school because he has received two C's, three D's, and an F. They have come to school only once each year to talk to the teacher who gave him his first F. This teacher, unskilled in parent interviews, told them bluntly that Jack was a very poor student and simply couldn't keep up with the class, that he never finished his work, and that what he did was inferior. The parents went home depressed and angry with both the school and with Jack. They felt that Jack did not have good teachers and that he was not trying. With Jack in the ninth grade they, like Gary's parents, have been invited to a career guidance evaluation and planning conference. Here are some excerpts from their interview.

Counselor: *How do you do. I'm Mr. Wright. Won't you come in? How are you, Jack? I'm glad you could all come in today. Jack and I are old friends, aren't we, Jack?*

Jack: *Yeah. I'm in here a lot 'cause I have so much trouble. School's too hard.*

Mr. Mitlock: *It wouldn't be too hard if you'd study more and if they had some decent teachers in this school!*

Counselor: *A great many of our students find school difficult even when they have very outstanding teachers. However, we are trying very hard to increase their interest by finding worthwhile work in which they can succeed. Jack does find his academic work quite difficult, but I wonder whether he has shown you the new book he was given to read on animal husbandry? As you may know, he has had some difficulty with his reading, but a week ago the librarian received a new book which is written in a simple, interesting way; I believe Jack is going to report on this in his science class.*

Mrs. Mitlock: *Nobody ever told us that he had difficulty in his reading. Why didn't he learn to read better in the elementary school? And why didn't somebody tell us he was having difficulty in reading a long time ago? Personally, I think he has had poor teachers right along and he still has! What's the matter with this school system?*

Counselor: *There are many reasons why children have difficulty in learning to read, Mrs. Mitlock. Sometimes, for one reason or another, they get off to a poor start. Something at home may be bothering them so much that they are not able to concentrate. Sometimes they have difficulty with their vision and no one is aware of it. Sometimes it is necessary for the family to move frequently. Sometimes there is a series of substitute teachers or a poor teacher. Then, of course, there is always the fact that reading and other academic subjects just come very hard for some children. But let us look at some of Jack's test results, his grades, what he has indicated as his interests, and then we can plan ahead better.* (Takes out Jack's test profile.)

Mr. Mitlock: *Where did you get all those numbers? Is that what you call a chart?*

Counselor: *Yes, you could call it that. We often call it a profile. This one has to do with interest. Jack has indicated by his answers in the test that he is most interested in work that would take him outdoors. You understand that this is only one indication of what he might be interested in. I wouldn't be too surprised, however, if he really does prefer being outdoors. How about it, Jack? Weren't you telling me last week that you had a wonderful time last summer when you were with your parents at your uncle's farm?*

Jack: *Yeah, I'll say!*

Mrs. Mitlock: *Yes. We all had a wonderful time, and we could hardly get Jack away from there. He wanted to stay with my brother and help him for the rest of the summer, but we felt he should come home with us. I wish we could get him that interested in his schoolwork!*

Counselor: *Sometimes it is hard to be interested in things we find difficult to do. You see from Jack's record here that he has found it difficult to make good grades all through school so far.*

Mr. Mitlock: *Well, he's going to have to do better. I want him to go on to school. We thought we would send him on to the junior college first and then see what we should do next.*

Counselor: *That is something to think about, but perhaps we should explore a little further. Jack has taken three scholastic-aptitude tests; one in the third grade, one in the fifth grade, and one in the seventh grade. Each one of these tests indicates that Jack will find academic work very difficult, but on his occupational-aptitude tests he has done rather well in some areas. Look at this score. It shows us that he has fine coordination. Sometimes I watch the students playing ball out on the field, and Jack more than holds his own. I'm wondering whether we shouldn't explore some ideas related to occupations in which he would have an opportunity to use his hands. Just as an example, we might think of the building trade or special work with animals. These offer many opportunities for a career.*

Mr. Mitlock: *Yes, I know, but I was hoping he would take a couple of years at junior college and maybe be an accountant. They make good money.*

Counselor: *Well, we surely don't need to rule that out. I suggested the building trade only because it offers so many opportunities, particularly at the present time, and because it represents the kind of thing that fits in somewhat with Jack's test results. And, of course, if Jack thoroughly enjoyed helping his uncle on the farm, we shouldn't overlook that either.*

Jack: *Boy, that's what I'd really like to do.*

Counselor: *Well, you know farming, building, and the many jobs connected with them are all highly respected and frequently pay very well. Certainly their contribution to our society is very important. What would you think if Jack explored these possibilities a little more? We have lots of written material on both fields, and I believe Jack's teacher might let him use either one or both in his project for his occupational unit.*

Mrs. Mitlock: *I have no objection to his exploring them, but he's going to go to college, I hope. By then, he probably will have changed his mind about this outdoor kind of work.*

Counselor: *This is possible, but let's not push him too hard. There's a happy medium in the amount of pressure that's best for a child. There can be too little or too much. Some youngsters work better when there isn't too much pressure. Thank you all so much for coming in. And, Jack, any time you want to come in and talk this over further with me, you know that you're always welcome.*

Jack: *Thanks. I'd rather come in for that than for the usual reason!*

Obviously, this is just a summary of a long conference in which much feeling against the school was expressed by the parents, who blamed the personnel for Jack's troubles; from the excerpts we have here, let's evaluate what the counselor actually did.

FIRST   When the father snapped at Jack that his work wouldn't be so hard if he studied more and if he had had good teachers, the counselor eased the situation by saying that many children find school difficult even when they have outstanding teachers. This took the pressure off Jack and actually off the teachers too.

SECOND   He was honest in saying that Jack *did* find academic work difficult, particularly in reading. Then, when Mrs. Mitlock became indignant about not having been told about Jack's reading difficulty and why he hadn't been taught to read, he ignored her criticism of the school and attempted to give plausible reasons why many children find reading difficult, finally putting his finger on the real reason. This was done in a kindly way.

THIRD   He led them into an examination of Jack's record, pointing out, first of all, that it appeared that Jack seemed most interested in the outdoors. This, then, led to a discussion of some of the opportunities therein.

FOURTH When the father suggested college and Jack's being an accountant, the counselor did not reject the idea but suggested that Jack should first explore the possibilities indicated by his objective tests.

FIFTH He suggested tactfully that Jack might do better without too much pressure being put on him.

SIXTH He gave Jack a feeling of warmth and support in the way he left the door open for him to come back at any time to discuss the matter further.

Counselors seldom complain about vocational-guidance conferences with the parents of superior children. Their problem is that these gifted children are interested in, and have the ability to do, so many different things that it is difficult to sort out what is best for their future. With proper motivation and a proper attitude toward work and toward people, these youngsters stand an excellent chance to succeed in many fields. Since attitude is so important and since these young people have so much to give, Chapter 9 was devoted to them.

The school social worker

CHAPTER TWELVE

The school social worker as a resource The school social worker's general approach "Teddy doesn't want to come to school": an illustrative case Conferences with parents What really happened in this case? What did the social worker do? The case of Jim: in trouble at junior high school Data from the cumulative record Conferences with all concerned A review of what took place

Many times a teacher has in her room two or three children whose deep-seated problems trouble her a great deal because she feels unable to do anything about them. Even teachers who are outstanding and who have had much experience in dealing with emotionally disturbed children sometimes find themselves helpless to bring about changes desirable in these youngsters. This means that there is a real need to obtain the help of a specialist. We have already discussed some of the functions of the school psychologist. Let us turn now to the kind of help that the school social worker can give.

The school social worker as a resource

There is a definite trend for school districts throughout the United States to employ trained psychiatric social workers to help alleviate teachers' problems with emotionally disturbed children. These social workers have had two years of intensive training in a graduate school of social work. In addition to the psychiatrically oriented theory courses, their training includes two placements in positions where they use therapy with children, under close supervision. At the end of this time, they have attained skills which give them unusual insight into the problems of the children and their parents with whom they work and also skills to deal with the problems most effectively. They can be called upon, then, as specialists who can really help children and also the teacher.

The school social worker's general approach

Although there are many different approaches, the referral often works this way:

> The teacher, Miss Brown, has in her fifth-grade class a boy whose behavior baffles her. He says silly things that make the other children laugh and disrupt the usually good order of her class. When Miss Brown stops him after class and speaks kindly to him, he answers her rudely. Nothing she does to help the boy seems to work, and so she refers him to Miss Williams, the school social worker.
>
> First, Miss Williams has a talk with the teacher. In the course of the conversation, she finds out how long the annoying behavior has been going on, situations in which the boy usually shows it, what his academic strengths and weaknesses are, what admirable qualities he has, and similar details. She also asks whether the teacher has any explanation of the boy's behavior.
>
> Next, Miss Williams makes a home visit. From observing parents and child together, she may make some inferences about the parent-child relation. She encourages the parents to express their feelings about the boy and their other children, as well as to give information about his interests, activities, friends, and attitude toward school. As they

talk informally, the school social worker reinforces any of the parents' positive insights, modifies slightly certain expressed points of view that may have a detrimental effect on the child, and helps the parents to suggest one or two definite things they can do to improve the situation.

After the home visit, the school social worker again contacts the teacher to be brought up to date on the boy's classroom behavior, to interpret to the teacher what she has learned from her conferences with parents and child, and to help the teacher suggest several things she might do to follow through the insights she has gained as to the cause of the boy's behavior.

Before her home visit, Miss Williams has an interview with the boy at school. After establishing a relation of mutual trust and respect—this often takes several sessions— she encourages the boy to tell how he feels about himself and the home and school situation and what he thinks might make it better.

Thus by working with teacher, parents, and the boy himself, the school social worker gains a clearer understanding of the nature of the problem and the concerted action that seems to be needed.

"Teddy doesn't want to come to school": an illustrative case

Teddy is a handsome little first grader with dark curly hair, big brown eyes, and an engaging smile. He seemed to enjoy school at first and got along fairly well. Recently, however, his attendance has been sporadic and, as a matter of fact, he had been absent for two full weeks when he was finally referred to the school social worker, who was assigned to his school one half day a week. The nurse had reported that no illness was involved, and a telephone call from the principal urging the mother to get Teddy to school resulted in the mother's crying and saying that Teddy didn't want to go to school and that she couldn't persuade him; that she had brought him to the building, but he refused to go in. Following are excerpts from the social worker's report of the case as she brought it to a successful close. (Please note that she never saw the child, since she knew that almost all cases of school phobia stemmed from problems of the parents. In this case the cause was particularly obvious after her first conversation with the mother.)

Conferences with parents

11/6/62   Conference with Mrs. M.

Mrs. M. was cooperative and quite willing to talk. She reported that Teddy's father is a bookkeeper. The family is Jewish-Spanish; the mother's parents are from Turkey. She said that Teddy is the second child, having an older sister aged eight. The pregnancy was breech in nature until the sixth month, when the baby turned himself. The delivery was normal and labor short. Very important to this case was the fact that the paternal grandfather died the week that Teddy was born. The grandmother very shortly decided that Teddy was taking her husband's place and now called him her husband. This made him a very special person. He has the top spot among her thirteen grandchildren. The mother feels that he is extremely special, too, since he turned himself before birth and she had a normal delivery. She feels that he did her a tremendous favor by doing this. For this reason, and because he is such a charming child, she finds it difficult ever to say "No" to him. The husband feels the same way.

After she related that much to me, there was a long pause; then she asked whether I would see her husband at home. I said that I could, but wondered whether it would interfere with the dinner hour. After another silence, Mrs.

M. said that perhaps this wouldn't be so good, since she always waits dinner for her husband. As soon as he eats, he goes right in to watch TV, which she deplores. She is very fed up with this. He does put the children to bed, and she thinks this is very good.

11/12/62

Mrs. M. was on time, smiling. She said that Teddy had promised to go to school after she saw me. She hopes he will. I wondered whether it was still hard to say "No" to Teddy. She said it was awfully hard at first but better now. Yesterday he was playing with the garbage can and she told him to stop. He said he wouldn't, but she made him. This made her feel very good. I wondered whether it was just as hard to say, "Yes, you must do something." She laughed and said it was. She hadn't realized until that morning that she had always told his sister to get dressed for school but she had never told Teddy to.

She said she has worried a great deal about his school absenteeism. She never had any smiles until today, when she felt like smiling because she had begun to accomplish something with Teddy. I praised her. She then appealed to me to know what to do today. We talked about things she could say to let him know she intended to be firm.

11/21/62

Mrs. M. again seemed to be quite happy with Teddy's improvement. He had gone to school two mornings this week. She said she realized now that she shouldn't have chased him before. I said perhaps she did what she felt was right then, but now in the light of our work together she has another way to think about this problem. She nodded and said, "I confused firmness with discipline. I thought they were the same, but now I see how they are different. But I was so afraid Teddy would run away and this frightened me to death."

11/21/62

Mr. M. is a tall, nice-looking, swarthy-skinned, over-polite man. He talked hastily for about fifteen minutes, seemingly to avoid my asking questions. He was eager to let me see he is smart and has an important place in his lodge, where his friends look up to him. I accepted this, saying I could see he was important in his community.

He said that he hardly knew his father and hoped that Teddy, whom he adores, will have happier memories of him when he gets older. He, too, wishes to be firm with the boy, but finds it very difficult. However, he thinks his wife should not be so upset by Teddy's threatening to run away. He said he had run away once and enjoyed the adventure. He tells Teddy to go ahead.

We talked about ways he and his wife could support each other in being more firm with the boy.

11/28/62   Conference with Mrs. M.

Mrs. M. reported that Teddy's teacher had been changed. Teddy had attended school every day last week, but now was very much upset and would not accept the new teacher and was being a very difficult child. He asked his mother who took care of her now while he was at school. (She feels she made a big mistake when he was smaller by telling him to come and take care of the house. He apparently had equated "house" with her.) She managed this by saying, "I am a big lady now and don't need to be cared for." She is trying to direct her own feelings so that Teddy cannot use them as an excuse for his behavior.

12/5/62   Conference with Miss Cohen, Teddy's new teacher

Miss Cohen is brusque, businesslike, and firm. She said she had heard of the trouble about getting Teddy to school.

She had had some difficulty getting him to do his work but felt this problem could be solved. Tim tends to answer for Teddy and she has put a stop to that, saying, "Tim, Teddy has a mouth of his own. Keep yours for yourself." She asked for suggestions, and I merely interpreted to her the dynamics of the case. I also told her to accept Mrs. M. where she was, that she was making real progress with the boy.

12/7/62   Conference with Mrs. M.

Teddy missed only one day this week. He surprised her this morning by being ready early and announcing that he was ready to go to school now. She feels definitely that he is about ready to go full time. She was very happy about this.

She spent considerable time discussing her hostile feelings toward her husband, saying that it had helped to talk to me and "get it out of her system." She feels somewhat more tolerant now. Her husband was laid off his second job last week, and so he was home on Saturday. He wanted to have a nap, but Teddy insisted on a haircut. Her husband protested but finally gave in.

- She was concerned that Teddy insisted on wearing tennis shoes. She argued with him about this, but he refused to wear his regular shoes. The next day she thought of me when he was insisting on the same thing, and so she didn't let him wear them. However, she bought new strings for them because she didn't have the courage to throw them away. Teddy went to school even though when Timmy came by for him, Timmy had on tennis shoes.

The teacher had told her that Teddy was doing a little bit better work at school and was pleased that his attendance was better.

As she left me she said that Teddy had asked her if she wasn't going to go to school any more. She told him that he was a big boy now and that he could go to school without

NATIONAL COLLEGE OF EDUCATION
LIBRARY

her checking on him. She feels that she has firmed up with him again and hopes that she can continue though she finds it very hard.

1/4/63   Conference with Mrs. M.

She reported that things were going fine. Teddy had been attending regularly, and the teacher had told her on the phone that Teddy had continued to improve both in his behavior and in his achievement. She was very much pleased about this. Her husband had noticed a difference at home too. He said, "Gee, Ted sure has changed," when Teddy behaved nicely in the car. Mrs. M. said, "Of course, he has. What do you think I've been going to school to see that social worker for all this time?"

She said she appreciated the fact that I had seen her again after the holidays. She thinks she can get along fine now but hopes that if she should begin to weaken again, or if Teddy gives her too much trouble about going to school, she can call me.

What really happened in this case?

We find a charming little boy who, because he was born the week his grandfather died, became the favorite grandson, the grandmother referring to him as her husband. Therefore he was very special to an important member of the family. This, together with the fact that he was a breech pregnancy but turned himself before he was born, thus doing what the mother considered a great favor to her, made him particularly dear and important to her and to the father, too. This boy had an extra-special place, then, which not many children enjoy. Teddy, therefore, was in complete control of the family. He chose not to go to school mostly because it was more pleasant to stay home and have people dote on him; at home there was no competition with other children for an adult's attention. His mother spent most of her time with him. In effect, the mother was hanging on to him without actually being aware of it. It was the job of the social worker to help her to see what was actually taking place between this boy and his family, how he was controlling everyone, and how this was keeping him from attending school.

What did the social worker do?

FIRST She got a developmental history of the child to see whether anything in the child's physical background would throw some light on the situation.

SECOND She inquired into the family background to see upon what foundation the dynamics of the case might lie. It is not unusual for the skillful social worker to make it easy for the parent to pour out family background. In this case, because the father had scarcely known his own father, he was anxious to do everything for his boy; the mother felt Teddy was a very special child and was grateful to him; the grandmother had him on an unnatural pedestal. All this added up in the social worker's mind to the total conception of why the little boy was as he was.

THIRD She accepted the feelings of all the people concerned, not once being critical in any way, but merely letting them express their feelings about this unusual child.

FOURTH She acknowledged that they were worried about Teddy's refusal to attend school but wondered whether they really wished to find ways to "firm up" with him. The mother and the social worker talked at length about this, the social worker constantly accepting the mother's feelings that it took courage to be firm because she didn't want Teddy to run away or be resentful.

FIFTH The social worker let the mother express some discontent and anger with her husband for his lack of attention to her and his preference for watching TV rather than talking to her. This helped to drain off the mother's hostility and also perhaps to counteract to some extent her centering her desire for love and affection on Teddy.

SIXTH The social worker accepted the father's feelings of

need to impress her with his importance in his lodge and his community. She helped him to feel important in this regard and also in regard to the necessity of supporting his wife in being firm with Teddy.

SEVENTH She helped the teacher to know a little more about the dynamics of Teddy's absenteeism and mischief, at the same time giving her support in the way she was handling him. In the same conference she explained that it would be wise for the teacher to accept Mrs. M. right where she was and not to feel critical because Mrs. M. found it difficult to be firm with Teddy.

EIGHTH In all interviews, as Mrs. M. related what she had done and felt good about, the social worker gave her praise, and when Mrs. M. appeared to feel frustrated or helpless, she helped her to think through the kinds of thing that she could do and the kinds of thing she could say to get better control of Teddy.

NINTH After a full month had passed, she had a follow-up interview with Mrs. M. to give her a feeling of continuing support. At this time, she let Mrs. M know that she would always be available if she wished to call her.

The case of Jim: in trouble at junior high school

Jim is a fourteen-year-old boy in the eighth grade in junior high school. He is red-headed and freckle-faced, with a composite IQ of 116. He was brought to the attention of the social worker because of habitual fighting, swearing, and smoking. Following are excerpts from her report of the case.

Data from the cumulative record

Study of Jim's cumulative record and a long talk with the vice-principal made it evident that Jim's trouble had become much more acute in the past month. He had been caught smoking a time or two in the seventh grade and once, earlier in the year, in the eighth grade. He had had three or four minor fights in the fifth, sixth, and seventh grades, but no incidents of a vicious nature occurred. In the last month, however, he had been flagrant in his smoking, obscene in his language even to the teachers, and extremely aggressive in his fighting, to the point of hurting other boys rather badly. He had been warned repeatedly and suspended four times within the month. His mother had been to school each time and although she was outwardly cooperative and always vehement in stating that she wanted her boy to do better, that they were a close family, that she wanted to be a good mother, and that she would see to it that Jim would improve, nothing actually happened. One day, in a fight, he knocked out another boy's front tooth. The parents of the other boy were very much upset, and the school personnel were called upon to arbitrate. Jim's parents paid the dental bill, but at this point, the vice-principal and principal felt that I should have a talk with the mother and the boy.

Conferences with all concerned

In my conference with the boy, who was somewhat sullen in the beginning, I picked up the feeling that he was somewhat mixed up and, in spite of his manifested belligerence, a little forlorn and basically passive. The vice-principal and principal understandably did not share my views.

At the first interview, Mrs. C., a nice-looking, black-haired, blue-eyed woman of medium height, was tense, smiling, anxious to please, and concerned about Jim, but determined to make him do as she wished. She described the family as very close; they loved and defended one another. I said I could see her deep interest in her family, and I wondered whether she felt like defending Jim now. She quickly denied this and then said if he had done anything wrong, she wanted him to take the consequences. She laughed a little and said since her maiden name was O'Hara, perhaps she didn't take the view of fighting the school people did, but she had tried to keep both her sons from fighting. It did seem, however, that Jim recently was doing a lot of fighting for both boys.

To my question, she replied that they had found out about a month ago that her other son, Tom, had a serious and unusual heart condition and their doctor had referred them to the Palo Alto Clinic. I recognized the great strain she was under because of Tom's health and Jim's trouble at school. Mrs. C. paused and then said with surprise that she felt like crying. I said perhaps she had many things to make her feel like crying. She said, "No, no, I never cry, and we must get to Jim's troubles." I said perhaps at another time we might talk about things that troubled her. She said she would like to come again next week.

In conference with the principal, vice-principal, and counselor after this interview, I speculated that Mrs. C. repressed her hostility, and since the other boy was quite ill, it was possible that Jim felt he had to act out for the whole family. I suggested that I see Mrs. C. several times and try to help her to express her hostility and cope with some of her overwhelming dependency needs. This would help to loosen the home situation a little, and so free the grip on Jim. I felt that this mother needed intensive treatment, and I thought my goal should be to get her to a psychiatric clinic. The family could not afford private help.

In my next interview, Mrs. C. talked about how much her family meant to her, how hard her husband worked, and how tight a budget they had. They are proud that she can be a full-time homemaker. She described her many economies. During this time, Mr. C. was laid off work and she became more anxious about their expenses.

She also chose to talk at some length about her own family history, saying that she hadn't known her own mother until recently because the mother had deserted her and her brother when they were small. Her father had made a play area in the back of his truck and had taken the children into the oil fields, parking the truck near the rig so he could watch them. When she was seven, her father remarried. Her stepmother was a good mother to them and they were very happy until she died. Shortly after this, Mrs. C. married.

Mrs. C. had always exchanged Christmas cards with her half sister, her own mother's daughter by a previous marriage. Her mother had taken this daughter with her when she had deserted Mrs. C. and her brother. At this point, she burst into tears and had a hard cry. Then she brightened up and said that she guessed she'd better put a smile on her face. I wondered why and said that maybe she didn't feel like smiling. Since she said she would put on a smile, I wondered whether she felt she wore this like a necklace. She laughed and said, "You don't even care if I don't smile?" I said I liked her however she felt like looking, that she could always be and act like her real self whenever she came to talk to me, that the inner Mrs. C. was perhaps a much more attractive person than she thought and maybe she needed to get to know her better.

I brought the conversation back to her half sister. She then related that this half sister had told her where her mother was. She wished to see her. Seeing her was a trying experience, and she found herself trying to please her now even in spite of the way her mother had treated her in the past. She feels a need to idealize the mother and becomes very upset when her mother vilifies the father, whom she considers to be a fine man. She then chose to speak of her little daughter Katie.

She considers Katie to be a gift from heaven. She feels that both boys adore their little sister, and Mrs. C. wants her to be the best and foremost girl in the neighborhood. Mrs. C. feels that there has been increasing trouble with Jim since Katie was born, but does not seem to have any insight into this.

Mrs. C. said that two weeks ago Jim threatened to run away. She handled this by telling him that he could not do it because then the family would not be complete; they must all be home together. I said it was sometimes very hard to accept the fact that the boys were growing up. Did she think that at some time they would need to go out on their own and perhaps leave home to do it? She seemed very surprised and said, of course, she wanted them to grow up and marry. I said she'd really like to think that they both might live in the same block then. She nodded slowly and admitted she had dreamed of that at times.

In the next interview, Mrs. C. said that her husband had become so angry at Jim that he gave him a whipping, the first time he had taken action. When I wondered about this, Mrs. C. indicated that she had given permission to him to do this because she had been trying to follow my suggestions. I brought out that my observation had been that she seemed to be trying to handle everything herself, whereas these boys really had both a mother and a father who were interested in them. I then wondered whether the whipping had helped Jim's behavior. She admitted that it had and also said that he had not been having as much trouble at school.

She said it was hard to share the responsibility of the children with her husband—in fact, almost impossible. She knew that she should, but also knew that she would need a great deal of help to let go her strong hold on the children. She reported that at my suggestion she had got an appointment at the psychiatric clinic so that she could do this and also get rid of the feeling of being "driven" to please everyone, including her own mother. She asked me if I would continue to see her until she was accepted in the clinic for treatment. I agreed to see her as she felt the need to talk.

A review of what took place

When the social worker was briefed on Jim's behavior, she intuitively felt that this boy, whom she considered to be basically passive, was acting out because of some recent development in the home. She based this on his past records, which were reasonably normal, and the rather sudden series of recent events. Her feelings about this were borne out as she worked with the mother. Let us see now how she operated and what took place in these interviews.

FIRST She established a relationship in which the mother felt free to talk in detail about her family. Through Mrs. C.'s emphatic statements that their family was close and she was determined to make Jim do as she desired, the social worker was able to pick up the definite feeling that Jim was being held in a tight vise.

SECOND She realized that this tense, controlling mother was extremely anxious to be perfect in her way of dealing with her boys, but in her very intense drive to do so, she was unconsciously forcing Jim to act out her own hostilities. Sensing these hostilities, the worker helped the mother to bring out her feelings about her own real mother, stepmother, and half sister.

THIRD The worker let the mother know that she was most sympathetic to her anxieties regarding her boys—Tom because of his illness and Jim because of his troubles at school.

FOURTH When the mother talked at length about the pride the family had in her being able to stay at home and be a homemaker, and her successful efforts at economics, the social worker praised her and gave her a feeling of real support.

FIFTH Since Mrs. C. was unaccustomed to crying, it bothered her to burst into tears in front of the social worker. It helped her immeasurably when the worker told her that she need not wear a smile as she would a necklace, that she could always be and act like her real self whenever she came to talk to her. The worker indicated that perhaps Mrs. C. was a more attractive person than she realized and that she needed to get to know herself better. This would give a person like Mrs. C. a tremendous boost and something to think about. We must remember that Mrs. C. had a tremendous drive to be perfect and to please everyone. Introspection here would be most helpful, and the social worker opened the door for it to Mrs. C.

SIXTH   It was obvious to the social worker that Mrs. C. never really wanted to let go of her children, and she helped her to verbalize this when Mrs. C. related Jim's threats to run away, by saying that it was sometimes very hard to see that the boys were growing up.

SEVENTH   While not indicated specifically in the report, an attempt was made by the social worker to help Mrs. C. feel that the boys had both a mother and a father and that perhaps she could let the father bear part of the burden of bringing up the children. With this help, Mrs. C. was able to allow the father to whip Jim when he needed it.

EIGHTH   Throughout the interviews, because of her sympathetic understanding of Mrs. C.'s overwhelming dependency needs, her feelings of having to be the perfect mother, and her repressed hostility (which the worker helped her to express), and through the skillful handling of Mrs. C.'s feelings, the worker gradually led her to have the insight that she would need psychiatric help to loosen her grip on her boys. Thus, they could make a more appropriate school adjustment.

There are thousands of cases in which the skills of the social workers can be utilized to help parents gain insights into their own problems; this helps them either to relax their rigidity, firm up their handling of their children, or change their own way of working with their youngsters; and this in turn can very definitely change the behavior of their children both in the school and in the home situation. Teachers should feel free to ask for their help.

Working with more expert persons or even reading about how they manage difficult cases helps the teacher to work more effectively with his own students. To be sure, the teacher does not have the background for gaining deeper insights about these cases, but the interpretations given by psychologist, psychiatrist, and school social worker often increase the teacher's understanding of many of the children and parents with whom he comes in contact. Such understanding will increase the effectiveness of the teacher's parent-teacher interviews.

Selected
references

I. Books and pamphlets

Brim, Orville G., Jr.: *Education for Child Rearing*, New York, Russell Sage Foundation, 1959.

Hymes, James L., Jr.: *Effective Home-School Relations*, Englewood Cliffs, N.J., Prentice-Hall, Inc., 1953. 264 pp.

Landau, Elliott D.: *Creative Parent-Teacher Conferences*, Salt Lake City, Utah, Education Association and Utah Congress of Parents and Teachers, 1960. 37 pp.

Langdon, Grace, and Irving W. Stout: *Helping Parents Understand Their Child's School*, Englewood Cliffs, N.J., Prentice-Hall, Inc., 1957. 492 pp.

———— and ————: *Teacher-Parent Interviews*, Englewood Cliffs, N.J., Prentice-Hall, Inc., 1954. 356 pp.

National School Public Relations Association in cooperation with Department of Classroom Teachers, National Education Association: *Conference Time for Parents and Teachers*, Washington, D.C., 1961. 35 pp.

National School Public Relations Association and Department of Elementary School Principals, National Education Association: *How to Help Your Child Learn*, Washington, D.C., 1960. 40 pp.

Osborne, Ernest: *The Parent-Teacher Partnership*, New York, Bureau of Publications, Teachers College, Columbia University, 1959. 52 pp.

Stout, Irving W., and Grace Langdon: *Parent-Teacher Relationships*, What Research Says to the Teacher, no. 16, prepared by the American Educational Research Association in cooperation with the Department of Classroom Teachers, Washington, D.C., National Education, September, 1958. 31 pp.

Strang, Ruth: *Helping Your Gifted Child*, New York, E. P. Dutton & Co., Inc., 1961. 270 pp.

————: *Helping Your Child Improve His Reading*, New York, E. P. Dutton & Co., Inc., 1962. 254 pp.

II. *Articles*

Bevans, C. F.: "Parent-Teacher Relationships," *School and Community*, 48:16, November, 1961.

Calatrello, R. L.: "Parent-Teacher Conferences," *Peabody Journal of Education*, 38:259–264, March, 1961.

Clark, Mrs. H. T.: "Home-School Associations," *Catholic School Journal*, 60:43–44, April, 1960.

Cunningham, D. S.: "How to Conduct Parent Conferences," *New York State Education*, 48:26–28, March, 1961.

Dalman, H., and K. E. Michael: "What Are Some New Trends in Reporting Student Growth and Achievement to Parents?" *National Association of Secondary School Principals Bulletin*, 44:146–149, April, 1960.

Daniels, E. B.: "Parent-Teacher Conferences," *School and Community*, 46:22, November, 1959.

Edwards, G. O.: "Coffee Cups Replace the Cracker Barrel," *National Association of Secondary School Principals Bulletin*, 44:68–69, September, 1960.

Fine, T. W.: "Parent Conferences in Junior High School," *National Association of Secondary School Principals Bulletin*, 44:104–105, November, 1960.

Grindle, J. L., and M. G. Douglass: "Hints for More Effective Parent Conferences," *Instructor*, 71:25, November, 1961.

Hanna, L.: "Teacher, the Tape Recorder, and the Parent," *Grade Teacher*, 78:62, December, 1960.

Hymes, J. L., Jr.: "Talking with Parents," *Grade Teacher*, 78:15, May, 1961.

Ingram, N.: "Adventure in Reporting to Parents," *University of Virginia Journal of Education*, 53:19+, February, 1960.

Johns, W. L.: "Guidance through Parent-Teacher Conferences," *Education*, 81:303–305, January, 1961.

Kimmel, Mrs. W.: "Home and School Must Work Together," *Illinois Education*, 48:109–112, November, 1959.

Kuhl, M. A.: "Work with Parents," *California Journal of Secondary Education*, 35:191–192, March, 1960.

Langer, M. F.: "Parent Groups in Total Family Therapy," *Children*, 6:69–71, March, 1959.

211

Mann, J.: "Guide for Parents and Teachers," *High Points*, 43:69–71, May, 1961.

Mustard, E. C.: "Case Study of a Junior High School Public Relations Program," *National Association of Secondary School Principals Bulletin*, 44:118–122, September, 1960.

Peterson, M. T.: "Teacher-Parent Intercommunication," *National Education Association Journal*, 49:13–14, December, 1960.

Rath, P. M.: "Parent in the Cooperative Program," *Journal of Business Education*, 36:208–210, February, 1961.

Reeves, K.: "Circle: Parent, Teacher, Child," *Grade Teacher*, 77:63+, February, 1960.

Roberts, G. D.: "Parent-School Relationships," *Volta Review*, 62:449–451, October, 1960.

Rogaway, B. J.: "Conferences with Parents of the Under-Six Child," *Childhood Education*, 37:275–277, February, 1961.

Ross, A.: "Home and School," *Times Education Supplement*, 2362:243, Aug. 26, 1960.

Rotholtz, A. M.: "Methods for Improving Parent-Teacher Relationships," *School Activities*, 31:108–118, December, 1959.

Sander, E. K.: "Counseling Parents of Stuttering Children," *Journal of Speech and Hearing Disorders*, 24:262–271, August, 1959.

Wertheim, E. S.: "Joint Interview Technique with Mother and Child," *Children*, 6:23–29, January, 1959.

Index

NATIONAL COLLEGE OF EDUCATION
LIBRARY